TWAYNE'S WORLD AUTHORS SERIES

A Survey of the World's Literature

Sylvia E. Bowman, Indiana University

GENERAL EDITOR

SWEDEN

Leif Sjöberg

State University of New York at Stony Brook

EDITOR

Hjalmar Bergman

TWAS 356

Hjalmar Bergman

Hjalmar Bergman

By ERIK HJALMAR LINDER

Translated from the Swedish
By CATHERINE DJURKLOU

TWAYNE PUBLISHERS
A DIVISION OF G. K. HALL & CO., BOSTON

Library of Congress Cataloging in Publication Data

Linder, Erik Hjalmar, 1906–
   Hjalmar Bergman.

   (Twayne's world authors series; TWAS 356: Sweden)
   Bibliography: pp. 187–93
   Includes index.
   1. Bergman, Hjalmar Fredrick Elgerus, 1883–1931.
PT9875.B53Z698   839.7372   74–23060
ISBN 0–8057–2147–9

MANUFACTURED IN THE UNITED STATES OF AMERICA

Contents

About the Author

Erik Hjalmar Linder, born in 1906, holds the doctorate in the history of literature from the University of Stockholm, where his dissertation appeared as *Hjalmar Bergmans ungdom* (Hjalmar Bergman's Youth, 1942). He had previously published *Hjalmar Bergman. En profilteckning* (Hjalmar Bergman. A Profile, 1940). Professor Linder continued his research on Hjalmar Bergman in two major works, *Sju världars herre* (The Master of Seven Worlds, 1962), covering Bergman's life and work up to 1918, and *Kärlek och fadershus farväl* (To Love and Home Farewell, 1973), discussing the following years. Professor Linder is recognized as the leading authority on Hjalmar Bergman.

Dr. Linder's most well-known work is *Fyra decennier av 1900-talet* (1949) which appeared as volume 8 in Schück's & Warburg's *Illustrerad Svensk Litteraturhistoria*. His book saw three new, revised editions, before it reappeared in an expanded version as *Fem decennier av nittonhundratalet* (Vol. I, 1965; Vol. II, 1966, 1185 pp.). In this unchallenged standard work on Swedish literature of the twentieth century Professor Linder, in surveys and separate essays on individual authors, provides superb characterizations and portraits of Swedish authors and critics.

In addition to the above mentioned works Professor Linder has published ten books of essays on literary and cultural subjects. His wife is the well-known novelist, Ulla Isaksson, who wrote the scripts for Ingmar Bergman's films, "The Brink of Life" and "The Virgin Spring." They make their home at Lerum, Göteborg, Sweden.

Preface

Hjalmar Bergman (1883–1931) achieved much success, especially as a novelist but also as a playwright. His works have been translated into many languages, and his significance has emerged more and more clearly over the years. But during his lifetime opinions of his work varied considerably. He was accused of regarding his characters with indifference, of getting lost in his own fantasies, of concocting black humor, of being a victim of pessimism. However, it was rarely denied that he was a genius.

These various reactions related, I believe, primarily to his exceptional skill as a narrator. His stories were full of unexpected events and impulsive human beings; the correct interpretation was not always easy to find. His characters could be viewed either psychoanalytically, i.e. as unusual individual cases, or as logical products of the community in which they lived. Which interpretation was right? Furthermore, his works had a philosophical dimension. The author suffers from a sense of being ill adjusted to "the world" and its laws. Life seems to him an ugly power struggle and a web of lies from which individuals must free themselves. This personal problem and its possible solutions are sometimes expressed in the form of paradoxes.

Since Bergman's death the criticism and research of his work have moved in different directions. Occasionally the dreamlike nature of his writings has been stressed, now and again the strong realism—and he certainly is a great *describer* of contemporary society. Some writers have underlined the symbolism in his stories; others have tried to see all his works in their biographical context. During the past few years, young scholars have viewed his entire literary production as an expression of conflict within bourgeois society.

As a result of this extensive research, much of what used to be regarded as obscure and bewildering in Bergman's novels and dramas has now become comprehensible. It has even grown difficult to see how some of the previous misunderstandings could have arisen. History has been kind to Hjalmar Bergman. His symbolic language seems no longer obscure but, rather, moving and expressive. In the context of later events, his pessimism and wit—and the two combined—appear neither provocative nor paradoxical; indeed, readers today would consider them well motivated.

I have tried in this book to do justice to Hjalmar Bergman's versatility. My analysis is separated into two parts. In the first, "Life and Fiction" (Biography and Symbols), I shall attempt to place his novels and plays biographically. My accounts will be rather detailed where the books in question have been published only in Swedish. In the second part, "Art, Techniques, Views of Life," I shall deal mainly with Bergman's "symbolic realism," i.e. the interplay between society, symbolic language, and personal philosophy (which one may sometimes call faith).

Naturally, I hope that my work will serve to make this remarkable author more accessible to non-Scandinavians and help to establish his place among "world authors" for an international audience.

ERIK HJALMAR LINDER

University of Stockholm

Chronology

1883 Hjalmar Fredrik Elgérus Bergman, son of Claes and Fredrique Bergman, born September 19 in Örebro, Närke, Sweden.

1899 Left Örebro high school.

1900 Matriculation (after private tutoring) in Västerås, Västmanland.

1900– Studies at Uppsala and Stockholm universities.
1901

1901– Studies in Florence.
1902

1904 Journey with Mrs. Fredrique Bergman to an eye specialist in Heidelberg. Another visit to Florence.

1905 *Maria Jesu moder* (*Mary, Mother of Jesus*, a play) published.

1905– Another extended stay in Florence. Visit to Paris.
1906

1906 *Solivro, Prins av Aeretanien* (*Solivro, Prince of Aeretania*) published.

1907 *Blå blommor* (*Blue Flowers*) published. Hjalmar Bergman visits Greece and Asia Minor.

1907 Engaged in June to Stina Lindberg.

1908 *Fru Wendla's kedja* (*Lady Wendla's Chain*) on stage.

1908 *Det underbara leendet* and *Familjens renhet* (*The Wonderful Smile* and *The Purity of the Family*, two plays) published.

1908 Married in August to Stina Lindberg. Moved to Lindesberg, Örebro county.

1909 *Savonarola* published. Moved to Rome.

1910 Spring. *Hans nåds testamente* (*The Baron's Will* or *His Grace's Last Testament*) published.

1910 Autumn. *Amourer* (*Loves,* short stories) published.

1911 Moved to Hälsingborg, Skåne, Sweden.

1912 *Parisina* (*Parisina*).

1912 *Vi Bookar, Krokar och Rothar* (*We Books, Krooks and Rooths*) published.

1912– Personal crisis. Illness.
1913

1913 *Loewen-historier* (*Loewen Stories,* three rather long stories) published. Journey to Germany and Switzerland. *Fru Gunhild på Hviskingeholm* (*Lady Gunhild at Hviskingeholm,* a short novel) published.

1914 Moved to Håknarp, Bröttjemark, Jönköping county. *Komedier i Bergslagen I: Två släkter* (*Comedies in Bergslagen I: Two Families*) published.

1915 Claes Bergman died. Hjalmar and Stina Bergman moved to Örebro.

1915 *Parisina* on stage. *Komedier II: Dansen på Frötjärn* (*Comedies in Bergslagen II: The Dance at Frötjärn*) published.

1916 Moved to Stockholm. *Komedier III: Knutsmässo marknad* (*Comedies in Bergslagen III: St. Canute's Fair*) published.

1917 *Dödens Arlekin* and *En skugga* (*Death's Harlequin* and *A Shadow*) on stage.

1917 A summer paradise found: Segelholmen, Dalarö. For several years his only permanent address.

1917 *Mor i Sutre* (*Ma at Sutre Inn*) published.

1918 *En döds memoarer* (*Memoirs of a Dead Man*) published.

1919 *Ett experiment* (*An Experiment*) on stage. Publication of *Markurells i Wadköping* (*The Markurells of Wadköping;* another English title: *God's Orchid*).

1919 Several film scripts and scenarios produced, among them
and director Victor Sjöström's international success *Vem*
after *dömer?* (*Who's the Judge* or *Love's Crucible,* in America called *Mortal Clay*). Released in 1922.

1920 *Herr von Hancken* published.

Chronology

1920– First postwar visit to southern Europe (Rome, Florence).
1921

1921 *Farmor och Vår Herre* (*Grandma and The Good Lord*; another English title: *Thy Rod and Thy Staff*) published.

1922 Journey to Austria and Germany. *Eros' begravning* (*Eros's Burial*) published.

1923 Sicily and Florence. *Jag, Ljung och Medardus* (*Ljung, Medardus and I*) published.

1923– Three months in Santa Monica, California, as scenario
1924 writer at Goldwyn's.

1924 Back in Europe (Paris and Stockholm). Publication of *Chefen fru Ingeborg* (*Mrs. Ingeborg the Boss*; another English title: *The Head of the Firm*).

1925 *Flickan i frack* (*The Girl in the Dress Suit*) published. *Swedenhielms* produced in Copenhagen.

1926 *Jonas och Helen* (*Jonas and Helen*) published. Marital crisis. Hjalmar Bergman alone in Berlin and traveling. Serious illness follows. Return to Stockholm and Mrs. Bergman.

1927 *Kerrmans i paradiset* (*The Kerrmans in Paradise*) published.

1928 *Patrasket* (*The Rabble*) on stage. *Lotten Brenners ferier* (*Lotten Brenner's Holidays*) published.

1929 *Kärlek genom ett fönster* (*Love through a Window*) published. *Markurells i Wadköping* produced as a radio play.

1930 *Markurells i Wadköping* on stage.

1930 *Clownen Jac* (*Jac the Clown*) produced as a feuilleton on radio, with the author himself reading the catechism of the clown. *Clownen Jac* published as a novel. Illness.

1931 January 1. Hjalmar Bergman dies in Berlin.

Introduction

In Sweden, as in the rest of Europe and the United States, the last decades of the nineteenth century were marked by rapid industrialization. Though the revolution was not yet complete in Sweden, it nevertheless made its presence felt. People saw their lives changed by new inventions: the railroad, telegraphy, the bicycle, even electric light. The cities began to attract growing numbers of people from the farms, and several Swedish cities doubled in size between 1880 and 1900.

All this led to social ferment, new sources of friction between the classes. The aristocrats were caricatured in the press, old bourgeois families were elbowed out by upstarts, the impoverished working classes began to demand economic as well as political rights. The public dialogue intensified, often in newly established newspapers. Naturally, the trend was reflected in the literature of the day: The changes demanded attention, and injustices demanded that moral stands be taken.

August Strindberg (1849–1912) was Sweden's great man of letters in the last two decades of the nineteenth century. As a playwright, his influence was not inconsiderable; as a novelist, he became well known, at least in Germany and France; as a poet, he remained the exclusive property of his homeland (as is so often true in the case of poetry). Initially, in all his roles, he represented the voice of opposition, in religious as well as social matters.

With equal fury, Strindberg lashed out at lazy, self-satisfied civil servants and at greedy businessmen. Regarding himself as *The Son of a Servant*, he featured reformers and the oppressed as the protagonists in his writings. Emile Zola in France was a kindred spirit: Strindberg was a "naturalist." And his invigorating use of language and his choice of realistic and controversial topics shaped an epoch.

The contrast was striking between Strindberg and his elder colleague, Viktor Rydberg (1828–1895). A respected and important poet, Rydberg wrote a more stately and formal prose than Strindberg and was more strongly influenced by the Latin; he chose lofty topics from fourth-century Greece and a romanticized vision of the Middle Ages, often with the aim of portraying humanistic ideals. A radical for his time, Rydberg wrote flaming poetic accusations of the oppression and exploitation he saw burgeoning in his society, and yet the styles and attitudes of the two men differ notably.

Strindberg and a small group of his contemporaries comprised "The Eighties" in Sweden. He was acquainted with the members of the "Radical Breakthrough" in Norway and Denmark, especially its leader, the radical Danish genius Georg Brandes (1842–1927). Strindberg saw himself as a competitor of Henrik Ibsen (1828–1906) in Norway. Although he sought and found kindred spirits throughout Europe, Strindberg was always controversial: he was hated, and he hated in return.

In the last decade of the century, the tide turned away from Strindberg, from naturalism and the violent spirit of opposition. The same was true in other parts of Europe. It would take too long to discuss here the extent to which this ensued from a general reaction of society. But in the literary world the desire for reform had abated, social involvement alone did not seem to satisfy people's needs; clearly, certain values had not been taken into account by the naturalists and moralistically motivated radicals. In any case, Europe witnessed a series of Christian conversions among prominent writers. Topics of social concern gave way to ideas that were deemed to have a greater general validity. A new form of romanticism came into being. Under the label of decadence, it evidenced a pronounced interest in spicy exoticism, in perfume, in eroticism. Under the label of symbolism, it placed enormous emphasis on style. This trend had few direct counterparts in Sweden, though one may speak of a parallel movement.

Let us define realism as a way of expressing social reality as if it had an intrinsic interest and were worth portraying for its own sake.

Unlike its counterpart in France, symbolism in Scandinavia came to designate a way of describing reality as if it were solely a means of reproducing something *else,* e.g. "life," the "ineluctable condition," the "riddle of existence," "human beings themselves."

By this definition, the 1890s nurtured a large measure of symbolism, apparent in the works of a whole galaxy of significant Swedish poets. The representative and polemical Verner von Heidenstam (1859–1940) was the most remarkable member of the group, but his poetry was virtually untranslatable, and he remained little known outside Sweden. The same was true of Gustaf Fröding, (1860–1911), regarded as one of the greatest of all Swedish poets. But at least one new writer succeeded in breaking through the language barrier: namely, Selma Lagerlöf (1858–1940). Her works were translated into a great many languages, and she was loved in her day by children all over the world for *The Wonderful Adventures of Nils* and *The Further Adventures of Nils.* Yet the majority of her novels and short stories were written not for children but for adults. They are serious tales of good and evil, with elements of social insight.

Selma Lagerlöf typified these writers and these times in two respects. In the first place, she did not reject the social criticism of the eighties: she considered herself a radical, and she called for social change. Secondly, she, like the others, was attracted to less topical and less controversial subjects than her contemporary, Strindberg. Frequently she wrote of the region in which she was born and bred, of its historical traditions. But she also set her tales in countries that were exotic in the eyes of nineteenth century Sweden: Italy and the Holy Land. Patriotism, regional romanticism, infatuation with history, and exoticism were thus some of the elements in the neo-romanticism of the nineties.

She also wrote many legends, and some of her contemporaries were absorbed in a certain religious-moral involvement, or at least an aesthetic interest in religious moods. Many young writers of the 1890s tended to use a surging, rhythmic prose in their efforts to create "moods."

But the writer to undergo the religious conversion of the decade was no less than the naturalist Strindberg himself. In his own dynamic fashion, he followed the attitudinal change of the times. Later he claimed that he had led it, both with respect to his choice of historical topics and to his romantic-lyrical approach. And, indeed, he was a leader. Even though his newly adopted Christianity would not have stood up to inspection in terms of dogma, it nevertheless served as the foundation on which his most original works were built. *A Dream Play*—with its highly developed symbolism and profound treatment of moral issues, its concern with the laws of life—was a precursor of expressionism in European drama.

Hjalmar Bergman belonged to the generation of Swedish authors who turned twenty in the early years of the twentieth century. There were several of them; actually seven were born in 1882 or 1883. As children they had witnessed the breakthrough of industrialism; they grew up together with Sweden's cities. Their origins were bourgeois.

As adolescents, the writers who were turning twenty in 1902 or 1903 had experienced the altercations involving Strindberg. They could remember his naturalism, but they had matured during the "new directions" of the nineties. Although compelled to admire Strindberg's genius, they could not mount the barricades in the manner of the eighties. It was hand in hand with the new romanticism that they took their first literary steps; they were tempted by both decadence and symbolism but could not be held captive by the passion for "moods."

Like Strindberg, they wrote realistically and factually. Often they set their stories in the region of their origin, as had the writers of the nineties. And like their immediate predecessors, they did not protest against the established order. They observed society in the light of their childhood memories, and their approach was seasoned with humor rather than satire. Their collective contribution came to represent a broad, realistic portrayal of Swedish life as they knew it, often tinged with regionalism. However, the language of symbolism was not entirely foreign to any of them, and some came to search for the meaning of life with increasing fervor.

Hjalmar Bergman was by far the greatest writer in this group. More of a spectator than his contemporaries, he observed life from the sidelines and seldom played an active part. At the same time, his fantasy seemed to know no bounds, and these two traits gave him his special quality. He was a man of insight, like Strindberg, but also a storyteller, like Lagerlöf, and he was influenced by both.

Although he cannot be labeled a symbolist, Bergman did create a symbolism of his own, in which the symbol was recognizable realistically but could nevertheless often be interpreted as a parable—a comparable device was used with brilliant success by Ibsen in his later plays. Nor could Bergman be classified as a realist, for his stories seemed to rely heavily on fantasy and frequently they open a new perspective on "life" and the "human condition." Nevertheless, his pieces can also be read as counterparts of real life: one observes social groups and classes struggling, competing, playing a game which can not only be recognized but which can also be fit easily into the social processes that dominated the century: industrialization and democratization.

Personally, Bergman came closest to being a conservative, but his stories show an understanding of power struggle and financial gain: social reformers have found insights as well as arguments in his material.

The same can probably be said of numerous European writers of the period: John Galsworthy in England, who was older than Bergman, and Roger Martin du Gard in France, who was almost the same age. But if parallels are to be drawn, the most rewarding comparison is with the American, William Faulkner. In certain respects, Bergman might be called Sweden's Faulkner —though Bergman was fourteen years older.

The similarity may be partially attributed to common literary influences. Bergman followed the example of Honoré de Balzac when he portrayed, in one novel after another, the same families and individuals from different perspectives. Faulkner was also a great admirer of Balzac and used the same device.

But the most striking similarity between Bergman and Faulkner lies in their creation of a single town and regional culture that reappear in book after book. The town is fictitious, with a fictitious name. Faulkner called his town "Jefferson" in "Yoknapatawpha County"; Bergman's is called "Wadköping" in "Bergslagen." Both towns are small, reflecting every aspect of human existence. In reality the counterpart of Jefferson was Faulkner's hometown of Oxford, Mississippi; the model for Wadköping was Bergman's birthplace, Örebro, in the province of Närke.

Jefferson, like Wadköping, is the scene of a struggle between the educated, prosperous families who have long dominated the town and the despised newcomers who demand power and influence. In Faulkner's *The Town*, it is Flem Snopes who, step by step, using every means possible, climbs the social ladder: finally, after great efforts, he becomes vice-president of the local bank and thereby achieves the status of respected citizen. In Bergman's *Markurells i Wadköping* (*God's Orchid*), it is H. H. Markurell, a wealthy innkeeper, who holds the fate of the whole town—and the future of Louis de Lorche, the prominent judge—in his plebeian hands; Markurell tries to win admiration and respect by donating money to the school and by allowing his son to study.

Markurell's discovery that he is not the father of his adored son leads to the climax of the story. *The Town* culminates in Flem Snopes's revenge for the same betrayal. Sex and morality in a conflict typical of the literary era!

The comparisons do not end here. The explanation of the similarities in these two writers' views of society must lie in the fact that Bergman and Faulkner—separated by an ocean and thousands of miles—grew up in towns which were at approximately the same stage of development and in the same semi-industrial culture; as young men, they experienced the beginnings of a cultural transformation under the rule of a new technology and new masters. Today the two towns are scarcely comparable. But they were sociological parallels when the two writers were children: industry was on a small scale, the towns were simply centers serving large rural areas and attracting people from the countryside. The framework of the inhabitants' daily lives consisted of a naïve and uncomplicated capitalism; moral and spiritual concepts were determined by a nineteenth century interpretation of the Bible: Oxford, like Örebro, was the seat of strong nonconformist religious sects with a fundamentalist emphasis. Principle and practice were often separated by a vast abyss.

Obviously, the differences were also considerable. There were no blacks in Örebro, nor any awareness of a racial problem. Faulkner was younger, with a consciously modernistic approach; he is often more "difficult" than Bergman. But both writers made frequent use of allusion, obliquity, and obscure association, and both have a kind of psychological humor that permits their characters to unmask themselves unconsciously and with comical effect; both occasionally remind us of Mark Twain.

But Bergman possesses a kind of wit, occasionally of a slightly academic nature, which was foreign to Faulkner. The mythical element is also stronger in the Swede: he makes use of extraordinary coincidences contrived with great ingenuity. It is also the source of the fantastic or even bizarre strain in his work.

Bergman was capable of ascending to a symbolical sphere in which deeds and words have double or triple significance; in which the clown suddenly becomes a prophet, the figure of fun becomes martyr or saint; in which the merry tale is transformed into either cruel tragedy or a mystery play between God and the soul.

Hjalmar Bergman once likened his fictional characters to silhouettes in a peepshow. To the reader, this comparison is highly inept: for silhouettes, they are extraordinarily vital and colorful. But let us accept it, for a moment. To conclude this introduction, and before proceeding to biographical notes and literary analysis, I should like to present three of the most remarkable "silhouettes."

Take the emaciated artist, Leonard Loewen in *Loewen-historier* (*Loewen Stories*). In Paris he has failed in love as well as in art, and now he has returned to his Swedish birth-place with scarcely a penny to his name. His only companion is a large cat, the model for his paintings of lions. Loewen is an outsider. He does not understand reality, yet he wants to change it. When he becomes aware of disputes, class differences, and tragedy in the tenement house in which he lodges, he wants to change things for the better, rather like a Don Quixote or a helpless Chaplin. But either reality won't *let* itself be under-stood (by him), or else it is in such a state of flux that it simply *cannot* be grasped (by him). A noble, helpful decision today is meaningless tomorrow. There is no one left who needs help. Reality is a phantasmagoria, a dream.

Or to take a more colorful and more strong-willed individual: The redheaded innkeeper Markurell in *God's Orchid*. He pads around in his stocking feet, has a crocodile's jaws: ill-bred, to say the least; and his harsh business methods have given him a bad reputation in the town of Wadköping. But his tough hide has a vulnerable spot: his boundless love for his handsome, black-haired son, Johan. The day he learns that the boy is not his own, his impulse is to lash out and commit murder. The primitive, the troll, the Leviathan learns the secrets of suffering. But revenge is denied him. Whatever he could do would cause irrevocable harm to the "lad." He is snared in a web of love. The rude boor achieves a kind of resignation: sometimes this process is called "coming to one's senses," or mastering the art of renunciation—Bergman's Swedish term for this state is *"besinning"* ("acquiescence" or "acceptance").

Let us look at the authoritative and domineering woman in Wadköping, Agnes Borck, or Grandmother in *Farmor och Vår Herre* ("*Thy Rod and Thy Staff*"). She longs for her grandchildren, wants to love and protect them. But when Nathan, her runaway grandson, returns home as a famous clown under the name of Jac Tracbac, her only reactions are disappointment, disgust, and anger, and their meeting results in great family battles. All her life Grandmother has loved passionately, but only through domination. She ruled her husband and her children, terrified them, and damaged them with her iron will; this she understands now for the first time. She would gladly have helped Nathan if he had been an impoverished circus roustabout (as he was when he ran away from home), but now that he is rich and famous, she throws him out as a stranger. When she finally begins to suspect the truth about herself and to realize that there are circumstances and situations beyond the grasp of her "good sense," she is destroyed. She arrives at a kind of insight and acquiescence (*besinning*), but by this time she is finished, her will power as well as her mind are gone.

These are examples of Hjalmar Bergman's stories. What such a brief outline cannot do is to convey the force and originality of the characters: Markurell, with his lusty outbursts, is a kind of sober Falstaff; Grandmother, with her cunning and despotic kindness, is the embodiment of all authoritative parents and grandparents; the clown and the artist, on the other hand, have special traits that make them the victims of the harsh laws of life, branded once and for all by fear (the clown) or by alienation (Loewen). They are extreme characters, but nevertheless reminiscent of certain literary prototypes.

Nor can a summary capture the stylistic skill and power of Hjalmar Bergman's stories, in which gaiety and a tragic sense of life are interwoven. Nor can it give an idea of the fertile imagination that constantly offers surprises and fresh aspects of situations the reader believed he fully understood. Hjalmar Bergman and Selma Lagerlöf had greater gifts of fantasy than any other Swedish writers. Nothing is too complicated for Berg-

man to write about; on the contrary, the tragic complexity of
life may be considered his principal theme. And he depicted
the absurdity of the world long before the term became a concept in literature.

The imagination of this versatile artist—who wrote novels,
short stories, dramas, comedies, and many film manuscripts, as
well as a considerable number of essays and speeches—was
sometimes a burden to him. He himself felt that his writings
were forced out of him by an overwhelming internal pressure.
As a rule he spent only a couple of months on a novel and two
or three weeks on a play while frequently a short story was
completed in two days.

In his private life, Bergman's hypersensitivity found two interchangeable outlets: aggression and fear. Two of his novels were
written about the clown, Jac Tracbac; in advertisements the
character was billed as a "Clown of Terror." The greatness of
this artist lay in his ability to portray fear; but in order to create
a truly comic sketch, first he had to frighten *himself* so that he
could play it perfectly, till his audience shrieked with laughter.
Hjalmar Bergman has him mutter: "Do you know what it costs
me to play the part? Do you know how much it costs? No, no-
body can know—except the person who pays."

PART I

Life and Fiction

CHAPTER 1

Childhood and Youth

PRACTICALLY all the realistic elements in Hjalmar Bergman's writings, a tremendous wealth of detail, originated in the world he experienced intensely as a child.

In 1914, following a consultation with a psychiatrist, he wrote an agitated letter to his wife. Here, too, he mentions his childhood experiences:

> I remember the days when I was little and built seven worlds, one on top of the other. What a job for a small boy between three and nine years old, to build seven worlds! You sometimes chide me for my laziness—but think what I have accomplished, how well I deserve to rest. . . . It was at that time that I asked my mother one day after church: "Mama, couldn't God be me?"
>
> And what was I in reality? An ungainly little boy, abnormally fat and clumsy. People laughed at me, children persecuted me. Have you any idea how many humiliations I endured during my first ten years? My heart had no shield. A glance or a laugh pierced raw flesh. So I had to learn how to retaliate in my own way.

The child Hjalmar Bergman was an obese little boy who preferred to play his own games with a small group of children whom he knew well. His fantasies about the "seven worlds" can be verified. Later his sisters spoke of the long stories he told about visions of a "higher world." Perhaps this was an escape from the harshness of the real world.

Hjalmar Bergman was born in 1883 in the town of Örebro in the province of Närke. His father was the head of a savings bank, a man of business. At the turn of the century, Claes Bergman was said to be "worth a million." His maternal grandfather was a prosperous burgher who owned a dye-works, and Bergman was tied, through his family, to the traditions of the town and province.

As if it were not enough that the boy was fat and ungainly, he was also the victim of merciless teachers, and he even came to believe that his nervous system had been brutalized during his first year in secondary school. However, it was surely no easy matter to handle this pink-cheeked, apparently robust, but thin-skinned boy (who occasionally, before going to school, suffered attacks of vomiting in terror of what lay before him). His isolation as a child was an omen of his subsequent, almost equally isolated life as a writer alone with his wife. An eye disease, which began when he was only twenty, also contributed to his isolation.

It is quite clear that Bergman's nature was profoundly disharmonious; this sometimes found expression in violent outbursts of rage. His obesity as a youth (as an adult he was a heavy but well-proportioned man) suggests an endocrine disorder.

Hjalmar Bergman's response to his childhood environment is closely associated with his relationship to his father, Claes Bergman. In the boy's early years, when he was regarded as "slow," he irritated his active, robust, and domineering father. This situation changed radically when he reached adolescence and it became clear that he was very gifted. Hjalmar became an object of adoration—if somewhat despotic adoration—and a source of pride. His father took him along wherever he went, including inspection trips to branch offices of the bank. In the novel *Jag, Ljung och Medardus* (*"Ljung, Medardus and I"*), Love (Louis), the narrator, relates:

Perhaps I wouldn't have submitted so unconditionally to his tyranny, his whims, his unpredictability, his sometimes incredible selfishness had not that same selfishness been balanced by an equally incredible goodness. What he did to others only they can tell, if they have the inclination. His concern for me and particularly for my health was touching to the point of absurdity and sometimes beyond it.

The boy Hjalmar Bergman thus accompanied his father on his travels during the 1890s. He even visited *Stora Sällskapet*, a club which met at the leading hotel in Örebro on various occasions, including St. Henrik's Fair, the ancient fur and iron market held on St. Henrik's Day in January. This market was a brilliant, belated Christmas spectacle in the eyes of the young people of Örebro. It meant crowds in the streets, flaming torches in the squares, parties in homes, and a sudden influx of visitors in whose conversations the word "Bergslagen" was frequently heard. Bergslagen is not the name of a province in Sweden, but a collective term for all the ancient mining settlements in the central part of the country.

In time, the festive crowd, the Bergslagen eccentrics, the anecdotes, and many of the outrageous witticisms from the *Sällskapet* meetings were all to be revived in Bergman's writings. The stories dated back to the period when the old Bergslagen was privately owned but in the process of being taken over by big, impersonal companies: dozens of mineworks were being shut down.

Hjalmar passed his matriculation examination at the age of seventeen. This occurred not in Örebro but in the neighboring town of Västerås where he took the examination, after studying with a private tutor, a whole year before his classmates. This episode has a special significance, and, from the point of view of family background, it is rather characteristic. Interestingly enough, it served as an act of revenge on the part of father and son for the boy's bad grade in German! Hjalmar had been failed in a German test when he had only two semesters left till the final examination. The grade was regarded by both Bergmans as blatantly unfair, and the youth undoubtedly scored a brilliant triumph in shortening his schooling by one year. On his return to Örebro, he was met at the railway station by his proud father in a flower-bedecked landau. Wearing his white student's cap, the symbol of success in his final examinations, the youth was driven through the town, his triumph presumably being observed by disgruntled former classmates.

The performance was carried off in true Claes Bergman style! It made an indelible impression on the boy of the significance of the matriculation examination in Sweden, and in his novel, *God's Orchid,* one central problem is whether the son, Johan, will pass the examination. Among other things, the novel reflects Swedish culture at the beginning of the twentieth century when the "white cap" was a class symbol and an unachievable goal for many; at the same time, the story was based on personal experience.

After his examination, Hjalmar spent a year at the University of Uppsala, and in Stockholm. His father intended for him to study something useful, but his plan came to naught. Like many other imaginative youths, Hjalmar was unhappy with the formal academic system and studied philosophy and aesthetics instead independently. The results of the year were nevertheless not too bad. He was tutored by Hans Larsson (1862–1944), a distinguished philosopher of the day whose writings on intuition are somewhat reminiscent of those of Bergson in France (though with a lesser element of mysticism). Larsson was a conscientious and sensitive scholar who was deeply concerned with aesthetic problems, and he awakened in his pupil a lifelong interest in Spinoza. Later Larsson wrote with great insight about Hjalmar Bergman's works, including the more difficult ones; his appreciation was undoubtedly founded on their early friendship, maintained by correspondence for many years.

Hjalmar Bergman left Uppsala in 1901 and in the fall of the same year departed for Italy to study art. There he found the city he would come to love above all others, the city to which he constantly yearned to return: Florence.

His first stay in Italy lasted almost six months, and it was during this period that he was introduced to the works of

Dante and Machiavelli (later he would translate *The Prince*). He also visited Florence briefly in 1904 and spent the winter of 1905–06 and the spring of 1907 in the city.

Then, in the fall of 1908, he married Stina Lindberg, daughter of the actor and theater producer August Lindberg.

The young couple first settled in Lindesberg in Bergslagen but moved to Rome only one year later. From that point on his whole life was regularly punctuated by sojourns abroad, and he found no permanent roots in Sweden until 1917, when he and his wife rented a summer home on a small island in the Stockholm archipelago, to which they returned every summer thereafter. Winters were usually spent in hotels, even in Sweden.

CHAPTER 2

Early Works

HJALMAR Bergman began to write when he was still a student, and his earliest extant unpublished efforts, two plays, reveal a vague idealism of a kind that was usual a couple of decades earlier, but that also recall Strindberg's wrestling with the Angel, particularly as expressed in the play, "To Damascus." These two plays were immature, but the youth developed rapidly.

Bergman's first book, written in 1904, was a biblical drama which, strangely enough, possesses some of the features of a passion play, *Maria, Jesu moder* (*Mary, Mother of Jesus*, 1904). We must bear in mind that the period was marked by theological discussions, including the question of the divinity of Christ; the play was an attempt to take a stand on this issue.

For the rest, the content and form of the early works were strongly influenced by the symbolical trends of the turn of the century. The pessimism they express, common at the time, was based on a reading of Schopenhauer. In *Mary, Mother of Jesus*, Mary was, in a sense, a rebellious superwoman with traits borrowed from Nietzsche. What is remarkable is that the individuality of the author emerges even at this point, though less in form than in content.

As already mentioned, the central theme of the work is a confrontation with the problem of the divinity of Christ. The basic ideas are borrowed from Viktor Rydberg, the Swedish poet, and from Ernest Renan (1823–1892), the French philosopher, but Bergman's psychological concepts are striking.

His thesis is that Mary, "the strongest woman in Israel," deliberately imbued in Jesus the belief that He was the Son

30

of Jehovah—this as a revenge on the priests and their followers for their persecution of her, the unwed mother. However, when Jesus, instead of serving as a tool of hatred, became another kind of rebel, a prophet of love, she experienced the disappointment of her life. She rejected Him at the moment of His death and, in her furious desperation, screamed with the crowd: "Crucify Him!" But she pulled herself together and soon, in order to avoid admitting defeat, it was she who brought the apostles the message that Christ was risen from the dead.... She is the "strongest woman in Israel."

Despite this secular answer to an ecclesiastical problem, the play is permeated by a youthfully romantic love of Jesus as a human being, as a symbol of good. The memorable characters in this lyrical drama include not only Mary, but also Judas Iscariot and Judas, brother of Jesus—a devoted, impulsive sixteen-year-old who was also bitterly disillusioned by the course of events.

Disillusionment is thus the theme of the first play: Judas Iscariot's disillusionment, the disillusionment of youth in the brother of Jesus. Mary, in turn, was a type to which Bergman returned time and again: the strong, sensible, self-assured character who one day discovers that she or he has misunderstood the deepest and most basic prerequisites for bold plans.

Following his debut, the twenty-one-year old writer began to experiment along different lines. *Solivro, Prins av Aeretanien* (*Solivro, Prince of Aeretania*) was a romantic tale of adventure with allegorical elements. *Familjens Renhet* (*The Purity of the Family*), on the other hand, was a response in a diametrically opposite direction: an exposé, a bitter "comedy" in the Ibsen style. The novel *Blå blommor* (*Blue Flowers*, 1907), at least superficially resembled a crime story from the naturalistic era (the 1880s in Sweden) yet is characterized by romantic symbolism with flowers and dreams, which bears traces of the style of the 1890s. However, all the works are concerned with the destruction of illusion.

What the young, innocent, romantic Prince Solivro discovers

in himself is not only treachery and fatigue, but also—what is stranger—an aggressiveness that is often ruthless, even a lust for murder. This lust to kill also has a covert erotic element, an element of sadism. Suppressed desires are symbolized by extinguished fires and by smoke.[1] Thus it is not surprising that the subject of *Blue Flowers* is a case of arson. The novel deals with half-conscious, forbidden desires that are partly incestuous and related intimately to violent jealousy. A number of dramatic episodes and conversations take place in the presence of a small boy named Ragnar—a masterfully drawn character—who has his own interpretation for everything that happens and who completely misunderstands the strange behavior of the adults.

In the spring of 1907, when Bergman spent some time in Florence—drawing up plans for a novel about Savonarola—he wrote two plays, which reveal that by this point Maeterlinck had replaced Ibsen as a direct influence on Bergman's writing. At this time the writer was engaged and anticipating marriage, and the plots of the plays relate to his situation. *Fru Wendlas kedja* (*Lady Wendla's Chain*) is a story of jealousy and cruel fate that is set on a farm in Bergslagen in the reign of Charles XII (1682–1718); the "chain" is a token of love and marital affinity. *Det underbara leendet* (*The Wonderful Smile*) is a fantastic version of the Old Norse saga of Vaulund, the smith, written in the suggestive, dreamlike style of Maeterlinck. The contrast between the latter play's Old Norse and symbolic elements has a strange effect. Here, too, jealousy is the basic motif. Vaulund strikes down his faithful wife in a fit of jealous rage.

Savonarola, an impressive work published in the spring of 1909, is the most important fruit of the young Bergman's Florentine studies. Subtitled *A Monastic Tale Told by Messer Guidantonio Vespucci,* the chronicle is a first person narrative. The Florentine monk's burning zeal is observed through the eyes of a man of admirably cool and ironic temperament. Vespucci, the narrator—a brother of the famous Amerigo—is a counsellor constantly on the move in the city; thus he is able to describe the reactions of both leaders and populace to the monk's activities. Bergman wanted to give a historically accurate picture of the times, and for the most part he based his story, almost in detail, on Pasquale Villari's great biography. Underlying the story of the remarkable prior—who for a few years was the most powerful person in Florence—runs a strong sense of boyish admiration for the prophetic force of the great preacher and, not least, for his "wrath." This admiration presents a contrast, in Bergmanian fashion, not only to the author's fundamental skepticism concerning the chances for improving the world but also to his own conviction that disillusionment and disappointment are the ultimate human lot. Readers unfamiliar with the Italian *quattrocento* may be a bit overwhelmed by the novel's infinite wealth of detail and fidelity to reality; to others more familiar with the Renaissance, the book comes off as a feat of magic.

Soon Bergman was to abandon his Italian themes. A series of short stories about contemporary Italy—some of them mature masterpieces—were published a year or so later in a volume entitled *Amourer* (*Loves,* 1910). Bergman next returned to the Renaissance in his play *Parisina,* written mainly in 1912, probably, and produced and published with some revisions in 1915. Its subject is jealousy: the aging Marquis Niccolo d'Este punishes his young wife for adultery. In Parisina and her lover Ugo, we find a link with the Tristan theme which had already appeared in Solivro (thus, with Bergman's first youthful romanticism).

As we have seen, Hjalmar Bergman's literary production as a young man was tumultuous: all his personal and artistic problems were struggling for expression. We find traits of decadence: for example, the toying with death, crime, and voluptuousness in *The Wonderful Smile* and *Blue Flowers.* Here are Schopenhauerian moods and other touches of *fin-de-siècle* pessimism (as in Solivro) but also colorful sagas, Tristanian romanticism, and historical atmosphere. In addition to

the disillusionment theme, the personal elements are the jealousy
motif, the analyses of rage and aggressiveness, and one or two
other motifs that might be called "semi-expressed desire" and
"love frustrated by inner resistance." Practically all are present
in *Solivro, Prince of Aeretania, Blue Flowers, Savonarola,* and
most of the plays.

Hjalmar Bergman himself had long been wondering about
the justifiability of a symbolism that "beautified" poetry,
creating an idealistic dream world. Life was merciless: true.
But was there such a thing as a useful lie, a life-lie, as a
counterbalance? If the romanticism in *Solivro, Prince of Aeretania* gave a positive answer to the question, *The Purity of
the Family* offered a purely negative response. Paradoxically,
Blue Flowers did, in a way, justify symbolism: admittedly,
life is horrible, but the floral camouflage of dreams and idealism
does offer a certain quality of grace that is essential to life.
Blue Flowers was prophetic in another sense as well. The
sinuous symbolism of flowers is incorporated into the realistic
plot in an ingeniously natural manner. In the same way,
Bergman, years after, was often to create a symbolic effect
without sacrificing realism. In his later works he made masterful
use of his great knowledge of external social realities to create
novels which could be called symbolical edifices.

His shift from romanticism to reality, around 1910, did not
mean that he turned his back on his innermost, most cherished
intention.

CHAPTER 3

His Childhood World as a Literary Source

HJALMAR Bergman entered into a new phase in his literary life when he and his young wife gave up their first home in Bergslagen near Örebro in the fall of 1909 and moved to Rome. Many circumstances may have played a part in this. His marriage and the sense of sovereignty in his own home gave him freedom; the sojourn in Lindesberg had brought Bergman into contact with the remnants of the old mining community and also with the countryside. But it was probably too reminiscent of his early life. Bergman was incapable of remaining long in one place, and the move to Rome provided him with a new and important stimulus. At last, he could view his home environment from a distance, and he now acknowledged (and sought medical treatment for) the morbid passion which was to obsess him throughout his life: jealousy. Consequently, his bitterness evaporated in the Italian sun, in the isolation that became possible in a foreign country. In any event, in the late fall of 1909 he wrote *Hans nåds testamente* (*His Grace's Last Testament*), a cheerful novel based on his impressions of reality—a significant omen for the future.

His Grace's Last Testament can be called a prose comedy— hovering above everyday reality, it may seem "light." But its ingenious plot, its sure, somewhat exaggerated characterizations and its agile psychology—even its depiction of the unpredictability of human nature and the consequent confusion of life— make it a genuinely mature Bergman work. The novel portrays the disillusionment of the young as they unmask the true face of adult reality, and it also presents the characteristic Bergman pessimism, grounded in the knowledge that young people are in the process of acquiring the hypocrisy of adults. However, what made the book a milestone for Bergman is that he had now begun using his childhood memories in his writings and was describing the world he remembered with good humor.

The model for His Grace, Baron Roger Adolf Abraham Bernhusen de Sars, Court Chamberlain and Lord of Rogershus Manor, was actually Hjalmar Bergman's godfather, eccentric old former Chamberlain Stedingk who owned an estate near Örebro. "Playing baron," or imitating Stedingk, had been one of Hjalmar Bergman's favorite pastimes as a child; the game was now revived in a festive novel, even though the gaiety had a tragic undertone. Stedingk had had a very countrified manservant about whom many anecdotes had been told; Berg-man endowed the gouty old baron in his book with the drollest of servants, a butler named Vickberg, a descendant of innum-erable manservants in Anglo-Saxon literature. However, the immediate literary impulse derived not from Dickens or any other Englishman, but from Fritz Reuter (1810–1874), a Ger-man author whose books Bergman had devoured as a boy. Reuter's novel *Durchläuchting*, about a duke in a tiny German duchy, inspired Bergman in his portrayal of the master of Rogershus. A new interest in humorous reminiscence had developed in contemporary Swedish literature (for example, in works of Ludvig Nordström), and Bergman had a wealth of childhood memories of his town and countryside upon which to draw.

As we see in *His Grace's Last Testament*, caprice ruled at Rogershus. The story is set in the reign of Charles XV (1826–1872) in the latter half of the nineteenth century—an epoch rumored by Swedish scandalmongers to be dedicated to frivolity—and the spirit of this age animated the life of the manor house.

Sixteen-year-old Blenda, the baron's out-of-wedlock child, lives on the estate as a foster daughter. Nineteen-year-old Jacob is the son of the housekeeper, Mrs. Enberg (widow of a minister), and of Toni, the Italian manservant. Later on it appears that Lovisa Enberg is also more closely related to her employer than her name and position suggest. This feudal confusion is seen in the novel through the satirical eyes of a bourgeois although the Baron himself is of good heart and head, of disarming spontaneity.

The central theme is the relationship between the two play-mates, Jacob and Blenda; Jacob is madly in love while Blenda, a playful child, scarcely understands what he is talking about (the character represents for Bergman an example of feminine fickleness). The Baron is preparing to write his will in Blenda's favor, but how and together with whom?

In one of the humorous complications the Baron's heartily disliked sister, the magnificent Mrs. Hyltenius (widow of a prelate), makes a claim on the estate on behalf of her own children; she wants either to have Blenda thrown out of the house or else to see her affianced to one of her sons. Blenda's whims complicate this struggle between the old man and his sister. When the book ends, it looks as if Blenda's heart—and thus the Baron's wishes—has weighed the scales in favor of one of Widow Hyltenius's two sons, a young curate.

Jealousy, Bergman's ever recurrent motif, grows in Jacob; disillusion mounts in Blenda; fiendishly spiteful impulses are obeyed by young and old. Yet the story has a brilliantly comic inventiveness and an extraordinary fantasy that give the impression that the author knows much more about human foibles than he feels inclined to admit.

The novel stands as evidence that Bergman had by this time matured to the point of complete control of his medium. Partially under the influence of Maupassant and Dostoevsky, he now tuned his instrument to even greater perfection in a collection of short stories—one of them dealing with jealousy and several set in Italy—published in the volume entitled *Loves.* One might say that he "trained himself in reality." There is good reason to believe that he wanted his next book, *Vi Bookar, Krokar and Rothar* (*We Books, Krooks and Rooths,* 1912), to be a broad, realistic portrayal of a town. He subtitled

it *From the Annals of a Town,* and concerned himself not only
with psychological realities, but also with the economic, social,
political, and religious facts of life.

Hjalmar Bergman and his wife were still living abroad when
he entered into this test of talent, but soon they returned to
Sweden for a couple of years and settled in Hälsingborg on
the south coast. Life in a medium-sized Swedish town may
have revived memories of the Örebro of his childhood. In any
case, Bergman referred in his new book to events in *His Grace's
Last Testament.* The idea of reintroducing certain names and
characters from earlier books may have originated in Balzac's
La Comédie humaine. At any rate, this is what he did in almost
all his subsequent novels.

"The annals" dealt with a town not far from Rogershus, and
the Baron and other characters turn up now and again in the
periphery; many details are rooted in local Örebro tradition.
At the same time, one cannot speak of an uncomplicated
"realism": Bergman uses a narrative style, and details, names,
and anecdotes pour out unpredictably as from the memory
of a well-informed but subjective story teller. The only discernible order is chronological, with the passage of years:
no single character dominates the foreground. It is the town
itself, its life and developments, that the writer tries to depict
as all the while his divining rod hovers over hidden spiritual
depths. The life of the town becomes a contest between wills,
but also the interplay between will and chance.

Old Man Broms founds Blekängen, a housing project for his
workmen, and spends his life tapping on walls and collecting
rents; he represents the capitalist class which the socialists of
the day so vividly caricatured as exploiters. It is evident that
the author's sympathies are with the poor: this novel shows
a society dominated by a middle class standing on the rim of
a bold new era. But Bergman's social radicalism had a patriarchal tinge. He regretted the decline of the traditional old
families (not unlike William Faulkner in his feelings about the
American South many years later); he is sympathetic to their

supremacy, and the great social reform in the book is implemented by an upper-class philanthropist, the softhearted engineer Krook. But Bergman believed he held no illusions about the nature of the world; he distributes criminals and hypocrites equally between the classes. He is furiously indignant at the high school teacher, Paulin (known as the Apostle), for his overzealous raids among school-boys to find evidence of vice, not to speak of the same man's oppression of his docile wife, Louise. Bergman is lavish with rollicking satire rendered in grotesque anecdotes about the Baron of Rogershus and the town newspaper. A keen observer, he describes the religious revival among the townspeople as a precursor of a social awakening, the imminent social revolution.

But it is difficult to decide which the author enjoyed most: playing with his sixty-three characters in fantastic miniature stories within the novel or developing his line of social analysis. The reader may sometimes lose track of the analysis in the flurry of events; but on closer inspection it proves to be extremely fundamental and durable.

The second half of the novel elaborates on Per's and Blenda's marriage, contracted in the earlier book. Per Hyltenius, now a settled estate-owner, is the eternal cuckold, hulking and lethargic. Blenda, his wife, still as capricious as at Rogershus, now takes her lovers where she finds them, and it is the erotic whims of the rich woman that ultimately determine the book's "happy ending"—the relatively satisfactory outcome of a social experiment.

Despite a myriad of destinies and characterizations, the book is finally a cohesive whole and an unusual work of art. Naturally, there is a bitter undertone to the basic concept, perceptible not only to readers of *His Grace's Last Testament* (who are familiar with the foibles of innocent, playful adolescents). Good will, according to Per Hyltenius, is found only in cold and quietly hopeless hearts. It is thus a matter of remaining detached from life—for one's own sake—almost in the Buddhist sense. The interplay of wills draws a picture of life that is apparently reality-based but nonetheless (or perhaps therefore) profoundly irrational. *We Books* . . . is Hjalmar Bergman's most powerful, large-scale realistic study, a work full of understanding for social process. It tells us, in a way I should like to call symbolic, what it is like to live and be human. The image suggests far more than it depicts.

CHAPTER 4

The Emergence of "Bergslagen"

THE years following 1912 were marked by a severe crisis in Hjalmar Bergman's life. He was ill and frequently consulted doctors about what he called his "spinal disease." He was unhappy in Hälsingborg and found it difficult to write. One cause of his depression may have been the fact that his great efforts at realism had not been received as he had hoped. (A leading critic, Fredrik Böök, wrote in a review of a "profound defect" in the author.) It is also possible that during this period Bergman gained greater insight into a side of himself that was not socially "acceptable": bisexual or homosexual interests which he had hinted at in symbolic form ever since his youth. His anxious insecurity about the significance of this dualism in his sexual instinct, and about its acceptance, caused him problems. Perhaps some of his terror, aggressiveness, and jealousy had their roots in this insecurity.

In any event, several years passed before he could bring himself to embark on a major work. The two books of the period, *Loewen-historier* (*Loewen Stories*, 1913) and *Komedier i Bergslagen, Två släkter* (*Comedies in Bergslagen: Two Families*, 1914) were collections of short stories written over unusually long periods of time for Bergman. Here he tended to concentrate on unsuccessful, neurotic characters in their relationships with strong, domineering individuals. The former he saw from within; the latter he drew objectively. The plots are often dreamlike and nightmarish, and the characters' obsessive, unpredictable, and absentminded behavior caused the critics to write of his "marionette technique."

As I mentioned in the introduction, Leonard Loewen, the

41

painter of noble birth, is almost Chaplinesque. The town he
returns to after being rejected by his Parisian mistress closely
resembles the anonymous town in *We Books*.... He is accompanied by his favorite model, a magnificent cat called
William Penn which he paints on his altarpieces as the lion of
Mark the Evangelist. Indeed, Loewen himself is also a leonine
character.[1] Brave and pure of heart, a Don Quixote, he hurls
himself into action to help many of the tenants in the tenement
house in which he happens to find lodging. But, as reality
proves unfathomable and strangely fluid, his actions come to
naught. When his money finally runs out and he lands in the
slum next to a churchyard in the story called "Thomei gård"
("The House of Thomeus"), his confusion turns to humiliation.
Loewen weeps bitter, compassionate tears with the helpless
Agnes, who is to be married off to a rich old usurer. Loewen
himself is drawn into the vicious and degraded atmosphere of
the horrible Mrs. Ekström, Agnes's mother. At last, the artist
is taken in by rich relatives in the Bourmaister mansion, but
"Gula huset" ("The Yellow House") the story of this episode,
is more superficial in its thriller approach.

While "47-an" ("Number 47"), the first story in this trilogy,
is an expression of confusion and "The House of Thomeus"
concerns humiliation, they are both bitter attacks on life.
Though both stories are based in reality, they are not told
for the sake of the factual material (as is sometimes the case
in *We Books*...), but only to illustrate the general nature of
existence. So it is understandable that the stories are dreamlike. The discovery of the treacherous way in which life
fluctuates gives rise to a sense of unreality. The inexorable
passage of time changes everything. What was important a few
minutes ago is now a bagatelle; yesterday's revolt answered
an injustice that is tolerable today or on its way to oblivion.[2]
Today's victim of injustice submits others to the same injustice
tomorrow.

It was from this depression that Hjalmar Bergman's Bergslagen emerged—with a very characteristic form of complex,

realistic-symbolical narrative. The real Bergslagen consists of hilly mining country extending through several provinces in Central Sweden, plus parts of the province of Närke (which is generally flat). In the Middle Ages, Örebro, Hjalmar Bergman's birthplace, served as the port from which Bergslagen ore was shipped, and the ore trade was still going on at the great winter market in Örebro during Bergman's youth.

But the writer chose not merely to "describe" or "analyse" Bergslagen, to reflect its customs and economy; rather, he made Bergslagen a symbolic area in his writings, a geographical concept which had little in common with the actual mining district beyond its name. The embryo of Bergman's personal Bergslagen appears in the masterly story, "Fru Gunhild på Hviskingeholm" ("Lady Gunhild of Hviskingeholm"), which was later incorporated in Part Two of *Comedies in Bergslagen*. Written in 1912, the story expresses many of the terrors of Hjalmar Bergman's existence: his fear of his eye disease, of insanity (a sense of unreality), but also his remorse about his own flight from reality and responsibility, his anxiety at having (in fantasies) confused duties with desires, women with men.

Once again we have the jealousy theme, and, strangely enough, the author (who in real life was the jealous one) identifies with the oppressed woman who dreams of the young lover she never had; the husband is portrayed as an aged despot. Lady Gunhild is married to an unattractive old man, Sir Abraham Lilja, and only in her dreams and fantasies does she encounter young Albrecht Bourmaister, the man she loves. She has borne several children, but when she finds herself pregnant again she hides away in a turret: there she dreams of the son she will bear (surely there can be no sin or danger in thinking about a son?). The son becomes the suitor of her dreams. But when the child is born, it is a daughter who is given the name of Judith, and Lady Gunhild returns to reality. After many years of doing her duty, however, she is once again seized with melancholy and, in her confusion, waits to be carried off by her lover. When her daughter Judith appears instead of a young man, she mistakes her for the male suitor she still (or once again) awaits: desire is confused with desire, dream with dream in the woman's soul, and the object of her desire changes shape as in a dream, the shadow of incest is cast upon love, and even the sexes are interchanged.

The stories in *Two Families* (Part One of *Comedies in Bergslagen*) are of same unreal, desperate nature—the term "marionette psychology" is not entirely unjustified. Bergman at this point abandoned Rogershus and the town as his setting and shifted to Bergslagen with its foundries and mines, posing as the capricious chronicler of the old estates in a style sometimes reminiscent of an Icelandic saga, sometimes of the writing of Selma Lagerlöf. Episodes gush forth from the depths of memory; they deal with injustices committed by powerful men, with brooding plans for revenge by the oppressed.

Often the stories dwell on disputes between fathers and sons who sometimes are forced to acknowledge that they are peers: equal in strength, in the tradition of the Icelandic saga. Sometimes the fathers commit acts of violence—as when Jan Erse, the bailiff, beats his son Erik to a pulp to impress his drinking companions. And occasionally the sons rebel or proudly assume their inheritance: estates, occupations, positions, and manners of being. Little Jörgen, in the story "Jörgen Siedels brev" ("Jörgen Siedel's Letter"), broods about his identity, his personal role in the long line of Jörgen Siedels; his brooding culminates in a mental breakdown, which is described in masterly fashion. Best executed is the episode which tells the story of one of the many men with the name of Jan Erse. All his life this one planned revenge on a certain Jörgen Siedel, a hulking, ruthless mine manager; his hate finally is disarmed when the two of them find themselves in mortal danger.

It is Bergman's brooding about himself, about his family and his relationship with his own father, that finds artistic expression in these strange and unforgettable tales of Bergslagen. Together these stories present a view of life that is gloomy and sometimes confused, and yet not without hope. Admittedly those with power fight for purely selfish motives, and the results are often empty triumphs, but their actions may lead to benefits for the community. The weak are sometimes sacrificed, often brood on revenge, but occasionally win an unexpected victory. Sometimes they are appeased by understanding the enemy and give in to chivalrous impulses. In certain respects this view of life is demoniac, obsessive, merciless, as when the malicious clergyman lures all the rats on the Ryglinge estate into the lake and after them the half-crazed Lady of Ryglinge, Fru Bolla herself. He does this to help the witch, Fru Beata Siedel, to take over the estate. This is a horror story, a tale of evil, one of the dark elements in the "comedies."

Hjalmar Bergman's father died in 1915. He had always been a source of generous financial support to his son, but after his death it was discovered that his assets were much smaller than anticipated, and so his son was compelled to abstain from his inheritance. It was now essential to Hjalmar Bergman for his books to be commercially successful. The death of his father was the beginning of an active, outgoing period: he personally approached theater managers, wrote a (not very successful) adventure book under a pseudonym, and deliberately attempted to be amusing in the subsequent volumes of the "comedies."

Dansen på Frötjärn (*The Dance at Frötjärn*), the gay and complex title story of Part II, borrows from both Selma Lagerlöf and *The Arabian Nights*. It is a tragic tale about Mrs. Barbro Backe, who stifles her love (a work with a concealed jealousy theme). In Part III, *Knutsmässo marknad* (*St. Canute's Fair*, 1916) the plot is a mad whirligig, an attempt to make the winter market in Örebro (associated with St. Henrik) a colorful and amusing affair.

In the book the market is named for St. Canute. At the particular market described in the story—the time was the middle of the nineteenth century—Jörgen Siedel is the victim of a murderer's knife. Thus death is present among the guests at the fair, who include members of many of Bergman's Bergslagen families: Bourmaister, Jan Erse, Brenner, Lilja. But a good part of the action is centered in the learned young schoolmaster, Ekmarck, son of the town constable. (Ekmarck also played the part of the seedy and alcoholic "cavalier" in *The Dance at Frötjärn.*) This time, as a youth, he experiences the disappointment of his life when he is jilted by his beloved Anna Brita, who marries Count Brenner, the rich old court chamberlain.

In this book, the leading lights of Bergslagen are assembled in town to do business, to spin yarns, and to enjoy themselves. But the streets and squares are teeming with townspeople, and the police sense unrest among the crowd. Pretorius, the juggler, fools the guards and sneaks through the city gate with his artists and girls to entertain the lower order, while an amateur theatrical company performs for the "upper ten" in Judge Norstedt's attic. Once again we have a cross section of a class society, but this time in a historical setting, viewed with a smile. Once again a showdown between the Siedels and the Ryglinge farmers, but fitted into a larger socio-economic pattern.

CHAPTER 5

A Creative Peak

THE success of *St. Canute's Fair* was a sign that Hjalmar
Bergman was on the way to regaining his strength. Only
a year later he and his wife found Segelholmen, the tiny, almost
deserted island that became their beloved summer sanctuary
and for many years their only permanent address. In the isolation of the island, Bergman seemed to find the calm he was
looking for, the solitude with his wife that he seemed to need.
One of his greatest novels was written during that first happy
summer on Segelholmen.

Mor i Sutre (*Ma at Sutre Inn*, 1917) served as a harbinger
to his writing of the 1920s; the chief character in the novel, for
example, is an authoritative, self-assured individual, the wife of
the inn-keeper. Its composition came to be echoed by that of
the better-known, later novels, *Thy Rod and Thy Staff* and *God's
Orchid*: apart from a short prologue, the entire action takes
place in one day. The same device was used in the first part
of *Blue Flowers*. But in *Ma at Sutre Inn* Bergman perfected
the narrative method he attempted earlier in *Blue Flowers*:
the latter work is a rapid, uncluttered sketch. Events are expressed almost entirely in dialogue and in brief "stage directions"; other essential information is provided *en passant* and
sparingly. Because events frequently are observed through the
eyes of the innkeeper's wife, the book has a sense of consistency;
dialect expressions and idiomatic speech are used to the same
end, but the delight and skill with which the story is told are
remarkable even for Bergman.

Sutre Inn in Bergslagen is ruled by sixty-year-old Mother
Boel, whose son is the proprietor. But her favorite son is young

Daniel, born when she was in her forties. The boy is in love with Valborg, daughter of the rich peddler Kling[1] who pays yearly visits to the area. Bergman's most profound characterization is devoted to Mother Boel; his most festive, to the pompous Kling whose booming voice habitually praises his wares in biblical terms.

Sutre is not a happy place. The innkeeper is unhappily married, and his stupid wife fills the house with her chatter about "Sutre's disgrace." For Sutre harbors what is considered a disgrace: little Basilius, raised with the other children, but born out of wedlock to the innkeeper's sister Stava—who is housekeeper to Count Arnfelt, the improverished and profligate lord of Frönsan Manor. This wretched creature, Basilius's father, represents a disturbing element of fantasy in the book; sometimes a leering Mephistopheles with roots in the medieval moralities, sometimes a sharp-witted thinker, Count Arnfelt explains the inner meaning of the book. Between him and Mother Boel exists a strange, secret bond of understanding.

This old and destitute Don Juan brings a young mistress to Sutre in the feared black wagon, used in the village in cholera epidemics. Wanted by the police for abduction, he has to hide. His arrival precipitates a whirlwind of events and mishaps over poor, defenseless Sutre—as, for example, when a group of starving lumbermen loiter around the place, seeing revenge on their employer (the Count) for unpaid wages. The outcome of it all is the murder of Daniel, the favorite son. An error, a case of mistaken identity!

Wise and warmhearted Ma, according to Bergman, is actually to blame for what happened. Once she had sent Stava to the Count in order to keep Daniel at home—even though she suspected what would happen to her daughter in the Count's house. With her secret burden of guilt, she is now incapable of throwing the Count out of Sutre. Her bond with Daniel is more than ordinary motherly love! She is jealous of Valborg. Deep inside, she confuses son with lover. . . . Just like Lady Gunhild. *Ma at Sutre Inn* is thus also a study in forgetfulness.[2]

She forgets everything she doesn't want to remember and see. But in a strange dream that comes to the old woman when she dozes off, seated on her bed, much of what she has forgotten and suppressed surfaces—dreams of her youth, stray desires, that live a twilight life behind the facade of the respectable matron.

Despite this revealing Freudian analysis, Ma at Sutre remains a character who inspires respect, admiration, and, ultimately, sympathy. Thoughtful, kindly, generous to the helpless and hungry who clutch at her skirts, she is the incarnation of motherliness—in Bergman's eyes. It is the intelligent gallows bird of a Count who expresses a passionate, if mocking tribute:

Incidentally, how is a mother's heart made? Of what? Of lust for power and desire to caress? Of sensuality and playfulness? What fire is it that burns in that mad sacrificial vessel? Love? Maybe so. But the word is ambiguous. The lust for life burns in my simple mechanism too. But it warms no one, hardly even me. I believe it must be Fire. With no attributes. Simply Fire without a name. Fire without aim. Fire without fuel. The Fire from which Fire was named.

The love Ma serves reaches deep down into the mystery of existence: it burns with the mysterious warmth of life, but it is also treacherous and dangerous. She loves Daniel and Basilius, but both are victims of this irrational game of love: we sense that little Basilius with his artist's soul has, in his vulnerable and lonely situation, already been frightened and branded for life.

CHAPTER 6

Grappling with Life

THE Bergmans moved to Stockholm in 1916 during World War I. In time this move came to represent a break from the deep solitude in which they had been living. Hjalmar was torn between his need for solitude (due in part to jealousy) and his need for relationships—he now felt an urge to be his own literary agent. Friction with the outside world was a frightful strain on his nerves, but he seems to have tried hard to free himself from the closed conjugal world he himself had created. At the same time, he appears to have perceived this as a betrayal not only of his wife, who shared the world with him, but also of the dreams of his youth, his own ethic of love—that is to say, of himself. Had this not annihilated his original identity? Was he not now already dead—though physically alive? This line of reasoning was discernible in the works of his youth and is related to the disillusionment theme.

All the while, the First World War was raging, presenting overwhelming problems for everyone.

Bergman sought support in philosophy: freedom consists of clairvoyance, renunciation, deliverance from instinctive, unrelenting assertion of self. The state one then achieves may seem either a kind of salvation, with biblical overtones, or a complete indifference to everything, annihilation with an undertone of desperation. But such freedom can also release a sort of gaiety!

Bergman's complex frame of mind at that time found rich and brilliant expression in the novel, *En döds memoarer* (*Memoirs of a Dead Man*, 1917), which I like to call the "watershed of his work," a parting of the ways both in Bergman's life and in his writing. (I shall analyze this novel in the last chapter of this book.) The title itself designates the subject: a man, a "corpse," looks back on his life and tries to chart his road to deliverance. But the story is ambiguous: from the ordinary human point of view, it is a tragedy, and the "deliverance" is only an almost unreal ray of light on the final scene, a hint of a promise, a rainbow.

The novel is also the history of a family and a slice of autobiography. Jan Arnberg, the "I" of the story, is the grandson of a bishop and has been raised in a bishop's palace. Here we have shades of the author's grandfather, who was not only a successful businessman and a millionaire, but also a pious and powerful old gentleman, whose churchly preoccupations led him to be known sometimes as "the Bishop." Life in Bergman's maternal grandfather's mansion, life with his Örebro relatives, is recreated here in idealized form, probably combined with visual memories of the Bishop's palace in Västerås, where Bergman took his matriculation examination.

Jan Arnberg can tell of a fateful deed, a murder committed by the first Arnberg (also known as Fält) which recurs in differing versions in later generations. It is a kind of curse. Is it the murderous curse of humanity? It calls for expiation by some member of the family; it demands repetition by another (like an obsession); it is escaped by a third through dedication to an *idée fixe*, a "purpose in life," which will replace the inherited obsession. The Arnbergs are an inoffensive if somewhat mixed lot, and their life in the town of W. or on the family estate, "—dal" ("—Valley"), which they soon lose, is described with subtle, intimate, sympathetic realism.

Glimpses from the United States of the turn of the century provide an almost hilarious contrast with the childhood environment. That country is described as an El Dorado for quack doctors. Jan's father, the inventor Johan Arnberg, lives in America, leads a hard life there pressured by bad luck and treachery, in the hope of becoming rich and buying back "—dal."

Meanwhile, the victim of the first murder was a Count Arnfelt (note the similarity in the name). Since that time a strange relationship had existed between the two families: Fält-Arnberg, the criminal, was the out-of-wedlock son of the count. From this springs a dual symbolism: The Arnfelts and the Arnbergs are *of the same blood*, but the Arnfelts are rapacious and strong, while the Arnbergs—all of them, with the possible exception of Jan's maternal grandfather, Bishop Julius Arnberg—are weak and doomed to destruction. Jan, who is weak, has an unscrupulous playmate: Mikael, whose paternal grandfather is a powerful banker by the name of Arnfelt. The bishop and the banker, both tall and gray-haired, are thus counterparts in the story—twins, so to speak—corresponding to Jan and Mikael, their respective grandsons. Jan and Mikael are engaged in a silent, bitter struggle. In a sense this struggle between strong and weak—a mirror for all human struggle—is a family affair between blood relatives; at times, it seems as if it were being fought within the same person.

The philosopher Hans Larsson, reviewing the book under the headline, "If All the I's Were One and the Same I," tried to trace the theme back to Plotinus. Another aspect of the symbolism is concerned with "illegitimacy": the Arnbergs are an "illegitimate" collateral branch of the noble family. Like the rest of the Arnfelts, Mikael "legitimately" belongs to the real world. Jan and his father, Johan, on the other hand, are 'illegitimate," alien, which in the book ultimately comes to mean unworldly. They are "strangers" in the world, the unworldly who long for deliverance—from the murderous will.

Jan Arnberg's "external" fate is decided when he falls in love with his cousin, Léonie, with Mikael as his rival. At first all appears to go well. In bigoted W., a secret tryst between the two young lovers inevitably causes a scandal. It is Mikael's intrigues that lead to disclosure.

Jan goes to sea and eventually lands in Hamburg. There, by various coincidences, he runs into a series of relatives, who in different ways remind him of the eternal presence of the family curse. Must not Jan himself fulfill his destiny? He sinks into apathy and finally winds up working as a handyman in a bizarre house of entertainment, where the nerves of the blasé clients are titillated by acts that remind them of death. The Hotel de Montsousonge is an anteroom to death, a limbo where everything becomes meaningless and where Jan finally has but one idea in mind. His only wish is to take his revenge on Mikael who—now an elegant, decadent roué—has taken over Léonie and become one of the habitués of the house.

Jan's guide in this world of death is a mysterious porter called Johannes—actually an unreal figure, the ghost of Jan's dead father. And even though the realistic illusion is never entirely abandoned, it is at his dead father's side that Jan finally realizes that life, which seems to consist of nothing but "musts," also actually offers the possibility of freedom. The crux is to see through one's "musts," inherited or acquired: they are obsessions, mechanisms, valid only for the person who has not penetrated to the very source, who has not learned the art of renunciation or of "dying."

Memoirs of a Dead Man is sustained by an extraordinarily forceful sense of fantasy—even though certain details in the symbolism lack general validity. In some sections, the book is a tale of suspense with ghostly elements in the style of Poe. In its bantering, realistic tone, the middle section, featuring a description of the town of W., anticipates the small-town satire in *God's Orchid*, which was written the following year. The conclusion is a mystery play with muffled, gentle movements, brilliant light, and biblically sonorous pronouncements from Father Johannes:

All are not alive who live; nor is death a gate that opens in one direction only. The Almighty shapes life according to His pleasure, and of death He makes a plaything. Our thoughts are will-o'-the-wisps, which please Him in their flickering play. But our wills rest in His hand. And when you feel that you are doomed under your own will, remember that it is in His hand, who revealed the bow of the heavens as a sign. Thus have no fear of your will, for it is not your tool, but that of Him who leads you.

Bergman's thesis is that people's thoughts are free, but not their will. Will is an act through which a predestined deed, or one determined by Another, takes possession of a person. In a letter to his publisher and friend, Tor Bonnier, Bergman wrote that he would like to believe in the existence of reason and good will, but if they did exist, they would be "treasures guarded under seventy seals somewhere in outer space."

CHAPTER 7

Three Farewells

IN one sense, *Memoirs of a Dead Man* was an admission of failure: "I don't belong in this life." In another sense, it was a declaration of independence: "I renounce, I have killed my will, I no longer obey the laws of life." But in still another sense it is an act of desperation and defiance: "I don't care what happens. I am prepared to die. Death is the only way out." All three interpretations should probably be taken into account.

It is clear that, beginning in 1919, Bergman achieved a certain sense of emancipation in his way of life as well. He began to go out in the world, to meet people as he never had before; he frequented restaurants; he made new friends, including young men whom he admired and to whom he sometimes became deeply attached. By the middle of the 1920s, this way of life had an element of desperation and self-destruction, which was later intensified.

In a letter to Hans Larsson, he wrote that the subsequent novels were "farewells": "In *God's Orchid*, from love and family life; in *Herr von Hancken*, from ambition and diverse utopias; in *Thy Rod and Thy Staff*, from the bourgeois environment of my origin." These words are confirmed by a detailed study of the contents of the books in question.

But there are many indications that their creation brought to Bergman a strong sense of freedom. Perhaps he felt that he had achieved an objectivity on life, the understanding of a "dead man." In some earlier novels, written around 1913, he seemed to immerse himself in the fate of his characters, to share their suffering, to experience the same sense of futility as they. Now comes a change. He sees Innkeeper Markurell in Wadköping from a distance. The whole of Wadköping, in fact, is like a miniature world, as though the author were the Creator Himself. One cannot help suspecting that the much discussed change in Hjalmar Bergman's prose style (beginning in 1919) derived from this new sense of independence. As artist Leonard Loewen suffered in 1913 from his situation as an outsider, Hjalmar Bergman suffered with him. The outsider Bergman, of 1919, exploits his situation as a masterly joke, philosophical banter, and his style becomes entertaining and witty. His intention was to give the impression of festive, stimulating humor. He wanted to preach what he had learned, pass on wisdom he had acquired, but in a light vein.

It is possible that certain financial successes had given him confidence and also an outward sense of power in his avocation. Victor Sjöström filmed *His Grace's Last Testament* in 1919, and Bergman was commissioned to write a number of film scripts in the 1920s.

In any event, the town of W. now assumed its full name, Wadköping, became the subject of satire, and the "Wadköping mentality" became a general concept, a popular term for human pettiness.

Like so many of Bergman's more high-spirited stories, *God's Orchid* is partly insane farce and partly psychological drama. Wadköping and its masters are described in cat-and-mouse fashion[1]; those who have just been stalking their prey will soon be hunted animals themselves.

Hilding Harald Markurell, innkeeper, deserves the epithet "Bergslagen troll" more than most Bergman characters. He is known for his fox-colored fringe of hair, his unscrupulous business tactics, and his hopeless love for his son, Johan. Someone once called him an "angel of hell"—an ancestor of his was hanged at the beginning of the seventeenth century. His son is to take his matriculation examination, and Markurell decides to bribe the examiners with a lunch and a donation to the school, in the hopes that they will pass the boy. The idea is blatantly unreasonable—although, in Sweden in those days, consideration may occasionally have been given to the social or financial status of a student's parent. But Markurell's show was staged with convincing bravado.

Bergman's description of the matriculation examination and of its vital significance to Swedish society and to the boy's advancement in the bourgeois world is a masterpiece of satirical precision. The lunch in the masters' committee room is pure farce. Yet the frightful spiritual suffering endured by the primitive Markurell—when suddenly he realizes that Johan is not his son—is profound psychological drama, rendered in comedy. The biological father is Judge de Lorche: lawyer, businessman, and a member of one of the "good, old families," whose financial fate is currently in the hands of the innkeeper. But Markurell's first thought is not of revenge. Wailing like Job perched on his upset safe, he has it out with God. Bergman can suggest profound suffering and violent conflict through the most bizarre effects. The redheaded innkeeper's almost animal passion for his offspring becomes deeply human. The story tells of a paternal love so great that it could triumph over the desire for revenge and over shame, jealousy, and arrogance.

As in *Ma at Sutre Inn*, the main action is confined to a single day, and it is played against a background of a Wadköping seething with intrigues, gossip, jealously preserved traditions, and more or less crooked business deals. Judge de Lorche, the distinguished and powerful embezzler and born gambler, and his wife, the "slender lady," provide a demoniac-romantic touch, a pale, frightening, and therefore very Bergmanian element in the apparently idyllic life of the small town. But they are surrounded by a myriad of characters whose behavior is marvelously funny. Only upon close inspection does one detect the other side of the coin of comedy: tragedy. The family life of Ström, the malicious wigmaker, is profoundly unhappy; he is oppressed and exploited by his rich friend, the innkeeper. The eloquent Mr. Barfoth, schoolmaster and glee club vocalist, is typical of the high-living Swedes of the days of King Oscar—

though Bergman does not conceal that he is also a poet *manqué* with a tragic case of alcoholism. Both lift up mirrors to Markurell to show him his true face, relentlessly forcing him to see his real self.

"A farewell to love and family life"? Yes, as Markurell's illusions of his marriage and son are destroyed. Markurell, powerful and self-assured though he may be, is goaded to the point of becoming a "dead man"—to the extreme limit of disillusion, the point of indifference to life and self-assertion when even the greedy learn to "renounce."[2] One of the extraordinary high points of the novel is Barfoth's biblical speech to his heartbroken friend: the parallel with the Book of Job is striking. In his speech he unmasks the lofty pretensions of the human ego and the need for humility.

Never, it would seem, has the absurdity of empty pretention, the tragedy of total exposure, been depicted with such masterly fury as in the next novel, *Herr von Hancken* (1920). (The surname is a play on the Swedish expression, *"hanka sig fram,"* to keep body and soul together as best one can.) This is the story of a miserable, unsuccessful member of the petty nobility on a visit together with his family to Iglinge Spa, near Wadköping, at the beginning of the nineteenth century. It is narrated, years later, by The Reverend B. B. Carlander, then a tutor in the von Hancken family. His notes provide a revealing and amusing pastiche of Swedish writing of the day—although Bergman also introduces more familiar picaresque traditions from *Don Quixote* and *The Pickwick Papers*. The Reverend Carlander has his own highly heretical "world theory." He believes that the Creation is a great game of solitaire, that the devil is God's devoted, useful handyman, who now and again shuffles the cards himself when his Master is taking a snooze. This theory is not unrelated to the author's own view of life.

Herr von Hancken has convinced himself and all the other guests at the resort that King Gustav IV Adolf is to pay a visit, so he proceeds to mobilize a gigantic organization to welcome him. But when the monarch fails to appear, Von Hancken is transformed into an uncompromising revolutionary. Royalist or revolutionary, he plays whichever role that happens to be more opportune. He, who, during his stay at the watering place, had claimed he was a count, divests himself of his imaginary coronet in a ceremony that literally pounds the strings of the reader's heart. The symbolism is thoroughly grotesque, as every single claim he has made has been a lie, a ploy intended to enhance his own importance. He is a total nonentity, but achieves dignity at the very moment he acknowledges his absolute worthlessness.

Thus he bade farewell to "ambition and diverse utopias."

Finally, the farewells to the author's own middle-class environment.

Thy Rod and Thy Staff (1921) was Bergman's most mature, most meaningful, and most personal work of art. His mercilessly dark philosophy of life is balanced here by compassion and insight. Grandmother, the protagonist—whose name is Agnes Borck and who was anticipated in *Ma at Sutre Inn*—is Bergman's most powerful characterization.

Once again a superior, strong-willed female character steps into the foreground of the story. Like Ma Boel at Sutre, Agnes Borck finally realizes that, while she might manage her household and family by using her own good sense, she cannot bend life to her will. She had misunderstood the ground rules and been living on illusion. Catastrophe, exposure, and her own memories are all that remain. "You must see yourself and make your judgement."

The story is told from Grandmother's point of view—not in the first person, but in her words. She reminisces and daydreams. She converses with Our Lord, who comes to her in the evenings and sits at her bedside. And thus the story is disclosed: The poor country girl marries the rich merchant, Borck, and finally acquires power over both him and his family. The others were so weak—she alone had a good head. She loved them all—but as a despot—and regarded her control over them as mere concern for their welfare.

But Grandmother is not the one to "take leave" of her environment; on the contrary, she is the *personification* of her environment, its dominant force. Like Markurell, she is compelled to
renounce, forced to "die." But circumstances here are something
else again. The character who knows he does not belong, the
one through whom "leave is taken," is her grandson, Nathan
Borck, the "illegitimate" outsider.

For there was a stranger in the nest, and this was the grand-
child she loved best (a motif from *Ma at Sutre Inn*). Her
favorite was nervous, timid Nathan, who ran away from home
and joined a circus. Now he is rich and famous, a clown and
film star, known in a later novel as Jac Tracbac.

The story has two climaxes. One occurs when Nathan returns
home on the old woman's birthday: contrary to Wadköping
expectations and common sense, he turns up well-dressed and
apparently affluent with no need for Grandmother's charity.
This deeply offends her. She has no words, no emotions with
which to love a person who does not need her protection. The
other climax is the big family scene, when the children tell
Grandmother the truth about herself: that she is despotic and
overbearing to the extent that she has crushed the spirits—and
love—of all of them, first and foremost her dead husband. (This
scene has counterparts in Dostoevsky.) The woman's lifelong
self-satisfaction is destroyed, a process that is sometimes interpreted in a religious light: it is the Lord who finally defeats
her. Ultimately she becomes "good," but—in accord with Hjalmar
Bergman's personal theory—at the price of total annihilation.
She is obliged to sacrifice her "good sense." It is true that she
and Nathan finally meet again, but in a world of fantasy,
memory, and make-believe: where, once more, he is a helpless
little child and she, the despot-mother, a teller of stories.
Reunion can never take place in the realm of reality, or on its
conditions.

The novel is extremely relevant to the author's own life. The
family environment is a new and ingenious variation of the
family situation in *Memoirs of a Dead Man*. Grandmother can

be regarded as a combination of two strong-willed characters in the author's childhood (neither of them women): one was his father, the other his maternal grandfather. But after his father's death, Bergman had transferred some of his youthful feelings of revolt—his need for a showdown—to his mother, and apparently it was natural for him to make the tyrant a woman. Nathan Borck, who creates a form of art from his own nervous fear, has many traits in common with Hjalmar Bergman: his unrest and rootlessness, his sense that people usually laugh at the experiences which to him were actually bitterly, defiantly serious. It is his own imagined return to his lost childhood—in the bourgeois world—that Bergman depicts, and it is the collision of orderly, middle-class concepts with the unpredictably demoniac nature of art that creates the tragedy. But what disillusions both Grandmother and Nathan profoundly is the treacherous inconstancy of life itself.

In its suggestive power, the book measures up to the Bergslagen comedies and *Ma at Sutre Inn*; as a complex, tightly drawn unit, it is a unique work of art. It also succeeds as an implicit analysis and critique of bourgeois society.

None of Hjalmar Bergman's later novels could seriously compete with the three written between 1919 and 1921. An interesting piece, for example, is *Jag, Ljung och Medardus* (*Ljung, Medardus and I*, 1923), a capricious book of memoirs, long sections of which are relatively cheerful. The persona is named Love Arnberg (Arnberg again!) and he comes from Wadköping. In the reminiscences Bergman surely came as close to the truth—at least in the inner psychological sense—as he could and would; this bitter and profoundly humorous book is extremely helpful in understanding the man.

On the other hand, *Eros begravning* (*Eros's Burial*, 1922), a collection of short stories framed by a tale about Bergslagen, reveals a hint of the fatigue that was beginning to possess him. Some of the stories are masterpieces, particularly "Hans Hinz and The Women"—a genuine Bergman (of some fifty-five pages). The style of the story that frames the collection is occasionally jocular, in an almost mechanical way. But the topic is note-worthy: a sudden recurrence and peculiar variation of the jealousy theme that preoccupied him a decade earlier. In this case, possessive, domineering jealousy becomes demoniac, continuing beyond the grave. An energetic young widow of a dissolute husband believes she has finished with love, once and for all, but suddenly she marries the manager of the estate she owns. This event, it turns out, was foreseen, almost in detail, by her despotic dead husband. It is as if he had been watching over her every step, even after his death. Eros is invincible: this was the lecherous old man's message, and he continued to preach it to his puritanical wife. Eventually he proved to be right.

CHAPTER 8

Later Novels of the 1920s

NINETEEN twenty-three may be regarded as still another milestone in Hjalmar Bergman's biography, for he spent the year in Taormina on the island of Sicily, and his work went well.

Toward the end of the year he went to Hollywood on an important screenwriting assignment for Samuel Goldwyn (whose firm had not yet merged into Metro-Goldwyn-Mayer). (The initiative was taken by Victor Sjöström, the Swedish director, then employed by the same company.) But after only three months Bergman returned to Europe, deeply disappointed. One of his manuscripts had been accepted, but others were either too expensive, too "European," or too "sophisticated." Furthermore, he could not put down roots in what he felt was an alien environment. Practically everything about Hollywood displeased him, particularly its tough commercial attitude to manuscripts and motion picture production. (Later, in the chapter on theater and films, I shall return to this period of his life.)

There is reason to believe that his drinking increased during and after the Hollywood episode. Upon his return, during a stay in Paris, his outward behavior underwent certain changes: he was no longer the correct, almost elegant gentleman he used to be. Sometimes he posed as "vicious" in front of his friends, and Nils Dardel, the Swedish artist, painted him as a slim, affected dandy. Although these changes were superficial, there is obviously a profound melancholy lurking beneath the surface: he longed for death, felt life was finished.

Bergman's next novel, *Chefen fru Ingeborg* (*The Head of the Firm*, 1924), is a story of passion with morbid elements.

The heroine is a statuesque, independent woman who is the victim of a passion she cannot condone, either morally or intellectually. A Ma Boel at Sutre Inn who nearly succumbs, a Lady Gunhild who can find no escape in dreams or confusion.

Fru Ingeborg is a widow and mother, the head of a dressmaking establishment in Stockholm. In her middle years, it becomes her fate to fall in love with her own son-in-law, the somewhat degenerate and impudent Louis de Lorche. With superb psychological insight, Bergman describes this self-disciplined woman as she begins to suspect the nature of her feelings, then denies them, then struggles, and finally is drawn to moral degradation. What is new here is his description of the way in which an upright woman in moral conflict faces a choice between victory or death. Suicide is the only way out.

"The small people"—the narrow-minded—do not believe that Duty and Love are stars; they consider them playthings. The great and serious-minded have quite another view. "When Love is in opposition to Duty, they see a sign that is an omen of death." Some critics[1] have claimed, with some justification, that Fru Ingeborg's voluntary death does not fit the framework of the story, is not an organic part of the whole. Others[2] have discussed the profound logic in the other symbolic events. They point out that fire and smoke, symbols of suppressed desire (often incest) recur throughout Bergman's works. In any event, *The Head of The Firm* presents, in a new and more radical form, problems that had long been worrying the author. He was deeply involved in Fru Ingeborg's moral tragedy. Perhaps he experienced his own tragedy as a moral one.

While Bergman occasionally used Freudian psychology in earlier works, he does so in this book with emphasis—almost pedagogically. The subconscious emits warning signals in dreams and slips of the tongue; passion seethes beneath the surface. Now and again he sounds like a psychology instructor reviewing a "case." The method is used with consummate skill, but not always to the advantage of the total effect. Stylistically, the book gives an impression that is wordier than that of almost any other of Bergman's works, but the characterizations offer the same profound insights, the plot has the same surprising twists, and the same visionary clarity is there. Louis de Lorche, the son-in-law, is a study in slippery, nasty humanity, a new and absolutely spineless version of the degenerate Mikael Arnfelt Bergman depicted in *Memoirs of a Dead Man.*

His novels from the latter half of the 1920s are extraordinarily witty and charming, particularly in the short, comic, and warm-hearted *Flickan i frack* (*The Girl in Dress Suit,* 1925), with its scenes from life in Wadköping, and the Paris novel, *Jonas och Helen* (*Jonas and Helen,* 1926), with its many delicately and profoundly humorous moods. But often this humor indicates a flight from reality—comedy may have been Bergman's built-in safety valve. In the story of the girl in the dress suit, the escape is to a Wadköping idyll (where basically nothing evil can happen); in the Paris novel it is escape to a myth about youth and innocence. And—as is often the case in Bergman's letters to friends and relatives—the lighthearted style is a protective device: he tries to tell his problems indirectly, with a smile.

In *Kerrmans i paradiset* (*The Kerrmans in Paradise,* 1927), the sequel to *Jonas and Helen,* Bergman's fatigue and inner disharmony are clearly discernible.

Lotten Brenners ferier (*Lotten Brenner's Holidays,* 1927) appears to have been written to repeat the success of *The Girl in the Dress Suit.* It features the same gay, chatty style—this time with an element of "academic" wit—but strain and desperation are blatantly obvious.

In spite of these inner tensions, it is evident that all these books were based on a philosophy, that they even carried a message. Increasingly, Hjalmar Bergman felt detached from life and its obligations; incapable of living up to his own expectations, he evolved into a wise moralizer, strewing counsel and admonitions all around him.

And his observations are not empty phrases. They deal with a concept that was first formulated in the play *Porten* (*The Portal,* 1921): rejection of illusions, achieving acceptance, *"besinning."* In a scene in a churchyard in *The Girl in the Dress Suit,* an elderly schoolmaster speaks eloquently about the insight required by old age. In the novels about Jonas Kerrman and his wife, Helen, compassion is the keyword. In these books his homage to youth has a tragic element: it is the tribute of a joyless man to joy, a nostalgia for the freshness and innocence of youth. Bergman never ceased to believe that "'we are born to be human beings, but age turns us into monsters."

CHAPTER 9

Plays and Films

THE fact that Hjalmar Bergman wrote more novels than dramas might imply that his plays were of secondary importance, that he turned them out with his left hand. Likewise, continuing along the biographical-chronological line, one finds that the novels are often exceptionally effective symbolic expressions for his life situation at any given point in time. With certain important exceptions, it is not so easy to find the same significance in the plays.

For the author himself, his playwriting was probably always more important. His first printed work was a play, and at the age of twenty-five he saw one of his plays produced at the Royal Dramatic Theater in Stockholm. Moreover, the performance took place during the opening week of the newly constructed theater in 1908. Thereafter he wrote one play after another, but while some of them were published, none was staged until 1915 when the Renaissance piece *Parisina* was produced successfully in the national theater.

Presumably, purely practical obstacles frustrated Hjalmar Bergman's growth as a dramatist for a very long time. It is true that he was sufficiently prolific to be able to write off an occasional play; still, he was too proud and active to want to write solely for the theater managers' bottom drawers. Consequently, novels and short stories became the outlet for his most important experiences and ideas.

The success of *Parisina* in 1915, nevertheless, was encouraging, and in 1917, after the death of his father had given Bergman a concrete financial motivation for writing, he once again began

writing plays and trying to launch them. These efforts resulted
in some of his most original dramas. With his *Marionettspel*
(*Marionette Plays*), particularly the one entitled *Herr Sleeman
kommer* (*Mr. Sleeman Is Coming*), he embarked on a new
course leading the way to the future: a suggestive, taut style,
a simple symbolical language and a certain sagalike symmetry
in the order of events. (A more detailed analysis will be given
in the chapter entitled "The Dramatist.")

But that future never materialized. Two of the *Marionette
Plays* produced in the national theater in 1917 were miserable
failures, mainly because of the director's lack of understanding.
Undoubtedly, Bergman took this defeat very hard; his wife
believed that it was one of the major disappointments of his
life. It is probable that the event caused him to put more
original drama aside and to try to woo audiences with conversational wit, in the manner of George Bernard Shaw—as in
Ett experiment (*An Experiment*, 1922)—or with exotic settings—
for example, in *Lodolezzi sjunger* (*Lodolezzi Sings*, produced
in 1919).

Two later plays which are more autobiographical—or, at
least, more intimately related to the problem complex in the
novels—are *The Portal* and *Sagan* (*The Legend*). The former,
with its expressionistic symbolism, preaches the doctrine of
acceptance, "*besinning*," which found so many suggestive expressions in the stories of the 1920s. *The Legend*, which Bergman relegated to his files, is written in realistic style, with an
admixture of sagalike ingredients. It represents the last appearance of the jealousy theme in Hjalmar Bergman's writing, a
final accounting with the love motif.

Hjalmar Bergman's popular breakthrough as a dramatist did
not come until the middle of the 1920s with the play, *Swedenhielms* (*The Swedenhielms*), in which, to the extent possible,
he abandoned symbolism, giving free rein to his wit and sense
of comedy. *The Swedenhielms* was followed by a series of
dramatizations, including *God's Orchid* and *His Grace's Last
Testament*, and also by several new plays. One was *Patrasket*

(*The Rabble*), which featured a Jewish theme—on the threshold of the Hitler era: it was a big hit on stage. But his most devoted admirers still find that his earlier works, from the years 1915–1923 (i.e., before he had his major successes in the theater) to be the finest and most durable; nevertheless, they were relatively unappreciated. Ultimately Bergman was truly successful in his courtship of the audience, but the price he paid was high.

His screenplays, to which his talent seems to have been especially well suited, were also eclipsed by this struggle. He first approached a filmmaker in 1917, probably for financial reasons. Surely the motion picture was an ideal medium for a man of such boundless fantasy! Bergman sent Victor Sjöström a long and imaginative manuscript, but the director is said to have replied: "Come down to earth, young man!"

Their collaboration, when it later materialized, was intense and successful. Hjalmar Bergman adapted his own and other authors' works for the screen and wrote original scripts which were directed by Victor Sjöström and Mauritz Stiller, two Swedish giants in the field at that time. His contribution, particularly the film, *Vem dömer?* (*Who's the Judge?*, 1922), undoubtedly played a significant part in the last phase of the heyday of Swedish films. It was work of this quality that led to his invitation to Hollywood in 1923—which, however, in his eyes resulted in an unpleasant interlude, if not complete failure.

Meanwhile, his health was probably seriously damaged by the time he returned from the United States in 1924. It is true that he continued to work on films—and subsequently for radio, the new medium—but he came to regard the results of these assignments as potboilers, and he could never overcome his dislike of the overly commercial attitudes of the motion picture industry. The era of grandeur in the Swedish film business was succeeded by a period of banality, when companies and directors tried to woo the international silent film audiences with worldly sham and sophisticated plots. Undeniably, Hjalmar Bergman contributed to this trend with one or two rather slick manuscripts.

His growing indifference to the world, and to himself, was clearly to blame for this lowering of standards—a manifestation of that inner state he called "death."

CHAPTER 10

Leave-taking

STILL another important date in the tragedy of Hjalmar Bergman's last years can be singled out: 1926. That year he became the victim of a skin disease which manifested itself in an unbearable itch; he consulted neurologists and heart specialists for the condition, which seemed to be a neurological condition. Finally it was accurately diagnosed by the doctors, but convalescence was both painful and protracted, and Bergman resorted to alcohol and other means to cure the intolerable irritation. This episode was a severe strain on his delicate nervous system.

At the same time, his desperation had already expressed itself in violent attacks of rage and in an intemperate style of life. True, summers were still spent on Segelholmen in relative peace and quiet, and for long periods during his travels he was able to maintain the isolation and balance essential to his work. But he was separated from his wife on several occasions and, during visits to postwar Berlin in 1925 and 1926, he appears to have made what may have been an ominous acquaintance with the indulgent life of pleasure to be found in the city in those days.

It was at that time that he formed friendships with Emil Jannings, the German actor, and Gösta Ekman, the scarcely less famous Swedish actor, who was then working on a film version of Faust. Ekman's volatile, gifted nature and his exquisite appearance fascinated Bergman. It was certainly no coincidence that the handsome, decadent new version of Mikael Arnfelt which appeared in the novel *The Kerrmans in Paradise* had traits clearly reminiscent of Gösta Ekman's personality, with its sometimes diabolical element.

71

Despite the disharmony and anxiety which now obviously
plagued Bergman, neither *The Kerrmans in Paradise, Lotten
Brenner's Holidays,* nor, especially, *The Rabble* lacked traces
of his power and originality. But by the winter of 1929, Bergman
did not have the strength to produce his usual annual novel.
Instead, he published a collection of short stories entitled *Kärlek
genom ett fönster* (*Love through a Window*). Quite unexpectedly, this became one of his most representative books.

Some of the stories are exquisite, others only brilliant caprices,
but in either case the pieces often deal with selfless goodness,
which once again is interpreted in biblical fashion. Here Bergman, the bitter skeptic, sometimes reminds us of Selma Lagerlöf,
teller of tales and believer in goodness. "Flickan och den listige
rövaren" ("The Girl and the Cunning Bandit") is an extraordinarily ingenious legend on this theme, and "I bonngårn satt snåle
Axelsson och mös" ("Stingy Farmer Axelsson Sat in His House
and Smirked") is a masterpiece of purely humorous good will. On
the other hand, "Ett lejon berättar följande" ("A Tale Told by a
Lion") actually consists of the roaring of a lion in parable form.
The story represents an unequivocal declaration that Hjalmar
Bergman *knows who he is.*

Bergman's significance as a writer of short stories is considerable, due to his ability to evoke vast associations solely
through occasional remarks or a brief summary of facts. (However, posthumous anthologies have not included stories that can
compete in significance with those he assembled in *Loves* and
Love through a Window.) Mention should perhaps be made
of the story entitled "Herr Markurells död" ("The Death of Mr.
Markurell"), which was published in 1941 in a volume by the
same name.

Clownen Jac (*Jac, the Clown*), Hjalmar Bergman's powerful
swan song, was broadcast in serialized form on Radio Sweden
from September to November 1930. It is an astonishing feat,
not so much for its fantasy and the forcefulness with which the
story is told (since the reader can scarcely go unaware
of a slightly mechanical touch here and there), but primarily

for the generosity and extraordinary self-understanding revealed in the composition of the book. By this time, Bergman had completely deteriorated physically. After the catastrophe of 1926, his need for artificial stimulants had steadily increased, and he was no doubt quite aware that his life was in danger. Or rather, perhaps, he longed for the danger to grow more intense. He was impatient for the finish. For he was already "dead."

That he was able, nevertheless, to produce a lucid, sharp, wise, and multi-faceted self-examination and analysis of his art—not to mention his analysis of different ways of life and ideals—must be regarded as an inexplicably brilliant feat. This document from the pen of a desperately ill and unhappy man bears not a trace of vengeance, no desire whatsoever to lay the blame elsewhere. It simply demonstrates clearly the reactions of a sensitive, imaginative, neurotic man to situations over which he has no control.

Jac Tracbac, the clown, lives an artificial life in his California bungalow (here, of course, we have the author's memories of his stay in Hollywood); he is more or less under the control of a powerful syndicate which organizes his films and his tours and manipulates important aspects of his private life for publicity purposes. In one sense, the clown is obviously Bergman himself; but not in another. While the major part of the novel is devoted to self-examination and a personal review of the past, the book also comes off as a deliberate satire on certain aspects of American life in the 1920s—or, rather, of modern commercial life all over the world.

Jac Tracbac, with his spleen and his occasional and unexpected recurrences of vitality, has many of the traits of characters created by Chaplin (as is also true of the artist, Loewen, in his time). The artificial and ostentatious elements in his environment, the many farfetched, entertaining publicity stunts arranged in his house and on his grounds, had their counterparts in the antics of other prominent American comedians of the day: for example, Harold Lloyd. Gösta Ekman's life and eccentricities probably also had some influence on the

creation of the clown's personality. Ekman had played clown
parts on numerous occasions and once acted the role of
Frederick the Great— also played by Jac Tracbac.[1]

On the other hand, the clown's dominant characteristics, his
nervous terror and his ability to transform his own reactions
into masterly art, derive from Bergman's own innermost experiences. The terror rooted in childhood had been mirrored in
his books, and only gradually did it recede into the background
as inspiration and motif. Now, in the moment of retrospection,
it is there once again.

Bergman was being personal and truthful in the choice of
a clown as *alter ego*. To him, poetry sometimes stood on the
verge of jest or of terror; jokes could sometimes be a combination
of terror and poetry, sometimes an end in themselves, but they
were seldom wholly absent from his speech or his writing.

The novel lacks *one* artistic quality which is otherwise present
in every Bergman product: a suggestive, joyful flow of narrative.
It is more sober, more expository, more unadorned narrative
than that found in any of Bergman's other works: hence, the
occasional impression of mechanicalness. In any case, this applies
to the capricious and macabre scenes between Jac and his
syndicate bosses, between Jac and his former wife (the beautiful
gypsy painter Siva Yala), between Jac and his Swedish nephew
Benjamin Borck, known as Benbé. On the other hand, there is
warmth and life and a dash of poetry in the events on the
Sanna estate in Bergslagen, close to Wadköping, where the
clown's relatives live: Mr. Längsäll, the solid, pious master,
and his calm, sensible wife, Lillemor, with their two daughters.
However, one of the daughters, the "odd," highly strung
Sanna-Sanna, is actually the clown's child by Lillemor, the fruit
of a moment of passion twenty years earlier. This is one of
the truths that emerges from the past during the course of
the story.

The clown Jac Tracbac—alias Nathan Borck from Wadköping,
whom we first met in *Thy Rod and Thy Staff*—still hopes for two
things in life. One is that Lillemor will remember him with

some degree of happiness; the other is that he will find in his daughter someone to cherish and love and will thereby rid himself of his hideous ennui and perhaps bring a breath of life into his desolate bungalow. Ennui, spleen, emptiness—these are the terms in which Bergman now describes the "death" he has been writing about for so long.

But things don't work out as the clown had hoped. A letter from Lillemor informs him that she regards their brief liaison "with revulsion in her soul, disgust in her heart, a disgrace, a filthy stain. . . ." This is a frightful blow delivered by the gentle Lillemor who, during the long years after her sexual encounter with him, had learned that people die but their actions live on. When his daughter eventually comes to California and turns out to be that Sanna-Sanna—with all the clown's eccentricities but none of his gifts—he understands he has nothing to hope for from her, either. The clown has no future, no immortality, no true life. "Stock sold out, going out of business. . . ."

When he finally faces the full truth, he sets off on his last, weird performance tour during which, instead of performing his usual sketches, he reads from a book his own "clown catechism." He tells his audience they laugh from cruelty; he calls his art "monkeyshines." The heart and soul of the clown are at stake. When the serial was broadcast in 1930, Hjalmar Bergman was allowed to read the clown's monologue himself.

The catechism glitters with all varieties of wisdom, malice, and bitterness and, especially, facetious and surprising turns of phrase; it enunciates many truths about the interchange between artist and audience, about the artist's relationship to love, about the purpose and meaning of clowning. "The aim of the true clown is to make the people know they are alive." In another context he comments that he can be proud of his calling "if a rattle of ridicule is placed in the hand of the clown and a crown of wisdom on his brow."

The clown's catechism also advised clowns to be humble. "For example, one can never understand a human being whom one despises." Members of the audiences are advised to carry a box of sympathy in their pocket at all times:

If you feel infected by anger, hurry up and pop some sympathy pills into your mouth. You will have a pleasantly cooling taste in your mouth, your headache will disappear and your eyes will brighten.

These phrases were commandments for Hjalmar Bergman himself. They give a picture of him as a writer. In the words of one Swedish critic, his tolerance in delineating his characters was enormous.[2] He observes the most impossible traits, the most revolting individuals, with complete objectivity, and this objectivity is perhaps the most remarkable aspect of his art— even bearing in mind his incredible fantasy and his pyro-technic explosion of ideas. His view of life was sombre, as is inevitable in a person who feels psychologically and physically handicapped, a prisoner of family and society, and who is looking for an explanation of the cruelty of life. But in his characterization of the great clown, in particular, he reveals a miraculous objectivity in his view of himself and his eccen-tricities. One might ask whether as neurotic a writer as Bergman has ever described his peculiarities so lucidly and against a background of such happy sanity. In this respect, Bergman differs drastically from Strindberg, whose psychic disposition often compelled him to see himself in the right and others in the wrong.

One sign of this extraordinary objectivity, this presence of mind, is that, when Bergman sensed the approach of death, he was able to plan and execute *Jac the Clown* and take a part him-self in its radio production. This must be regarded as the cul-mination of his life as a writer, as the fitting final act.

Hjalmar Bergman went to Germany in December, 1930, after he had himself broadcast the clown's catechism. He died on January 1, 1931, in Berlin.

PART II

Art, Techniques, Views of Life

CHAPTER 11

The Storyteller

AT times, Hjalmar Bergman worked exceedingly fast. His inspiration had a strong element of compulsion and was frequently visionary. In answer to a questionnaire, he once wrote that a poem, a drama lives "in space" long before it is written down on paper.

Outside events are only liberating or, rather, focusing agents. Let us take a few examples from my own works: *The Portal* originated from an episode in which I nearly lost my life, *Swedenhielms* from a flash of memory of an old woman [Boman in the play], *Death's Harlequin* from the death of my father. But it would be wrong to believe that the plays were based on these factors. They existed long before I, in my insignificance, appeared on earth. These events were but orders issued to me.[1]

He never felt compelled to refuse an assignment, he once explained, because he was "almost certain" that

I can always produce something. I don't decide in advance that I'll write about this or that. The theme is unknown even to me until the last minute. It often unfolds itself when I suddenly hit upon an introductory phrase. After that the story develops on its own without hesitation; I often have a feeling that I have no control over what I write. And that, of course, is comforting.

Thus it would seem that events, ideas, or memories would suddenly pop up and "insist on attention." At this point, the skeleton of the plot could usually be constructed in almost no time. *The*

79

Swedenhielms, he claimed, was outlined fairly clearly within ten or fifteen minutes.

Mrs. Bergman tells of a film manuscript her husband had been asked to write.[2] One morning Bergman announced his decision to write the script, went into his study, paced the floor for an hour or so, returned to his wife and told her his thoughts. She was unenthusiastic and, although he himself knew that the idea was worthless, he became stubborn and angry. He went back to his room, but within a quarter of an hour returned to relate the plot of *Who's the Judge?* (a film with a medieval setting) from the first to the last scene. One of the subjects of the film was a wife's plan to murder her husband.

I was completely flabbergasted when he had finished and asked him: "Where did you get all that in only a quarter of an hour?" He replied: "Well, I saw the monk and the woman standing by the fireplace in my room, and they were fumbling with something I couldn't see. But then I saw the ring the monk was holding in his hand. At that moment he opened the tiny secret compartment under the stone in the ring and put in the poison, as the woman told him to. And then the whole story unfolded by itself. Will it do?"

Hjalmar Bergman once wrote a fascinating account of his working approach to a play in a letter (dated December 20, 1912) to his teacher Hans Larsson, who had just published a psychological study of "Intuition." This serious but lively account reveals more clearly than the quotations above that inspiration and planning were not merely passive processes: they also included active elements.

When one embarks on a play, one is first enmeshed in the subject. A little distance is then called for in order to take a look at the characters. Don't introduce yourself to them, because that will create personal relationships and elicit artificial responses. Simply mingle with them as a stranger—but steal a glance at them now and then. And finally you will get to know them, or think you do. Then suddenly you go up to the hero, grab him by the collar, move him here and there, have him raise and lower his voice, watch his facial expressions, make experiments and counter-experiments. If your grip on him is really firm, you may even dare to say to him: "That's not very effective, say it another way!" You work with the entire cast, with furniture, with backstage activities, with lighting. A constant dashing back and forth on stage. You must never let the actors entirely out of your sight—no more than a tamer with his tigers. On the other hand, one has a certain aversion to riveting them with ones eyes, a sort of fear.

Then all of a sudden you come to a standstill in the middle of the stage. The dashing around was actually an unconscious attempt to find the *central point*. Now you are there, and now you are the *master*! You stand in the center of the circle, and there is not one point, one thing within the periphery that you cannot easily and quickly grasp and control without changing position. At that moment or those moments, the play exists as it will never exist again. In a flash—for an instant. A second later the point may often be passed and the periphery broken—more or less. That is why a play is so seldom—never microscopically—what it should be: a circle.

I believe that if, at this moment of intuition, one could ask the playwright for the tenth line in the seventeenth scene of the second act of the unwritten play, he would reply with the accuracy of a sleepwalker.

Thus he envisaged the workings of his imagination.

It is difficult to analyze the secret of a creative artist's fantasy. In some areas, however, one can occasionally point to certain characteristics that distinguish him from others. Hjalmar Bergman had a way of describing people or of breathing life into them that can be partially analyzed, and he himself provided certain clues to his collection of characters.

One of them is contained in a lecture in 1928[3] entitled "Caricature and Cliché," another in an essay written in 1930 under the title, "Örebro People I Know and Örebro People Who Are Well Known." The latter gives a hint of the way in which the artist viewed the world of his childhood. The former seems to treat aesthetic principles but in reality is a rather bold defense of his own approach. The convincing objectivity is actually simulated. Bergman is pleading his own case.

In contrast to the painters and writers who document what they have to say "with a variety of not especially concise, though credible terms," Bergman speaks of a "caricature" method, among whose practitioners he includes Dostoevsky, Balzac, and Michelangelo. Theirs is a method of radical simplification, exaggeration of certain features. On the other hand, in Bergman's opinion Goethe as a prose writer and Zola, both drew a picture through an accumulation of details that later caused the viewer considerable difficulty. For it is up to the reader to bring about the essential simplification, the summary, the synthesis. "In the caricature," however,

the burden is on the master; it is his entire responsibility. Just look at God's creation of Adam on the ceiling of the Sistine Chapel—the effect is not due to "credibility" but to the force of the gesture, the authority of the artist.

Bergman takes issue with the theory that it is a question of temperament and tries instead to prove that two distinct artistic principles are involved. But it is nevertheless clear that it is his own temperament, his impatience, his sense of the extreme that make him indifferent to what he calls "cliché art," art that is "credible" but does not achieve the more profound "validity" of "caricature art." It is the immediately convincing force that he looks for in each work of art.

He is most informative, however, when he discusses the relationship between "caricature" and memory. In reality, he says, our memory resembles a warehouse filled with caricatures— caricatures of people, things, landscapes, events, emotions, notions. One is aware of this when one asks childhood friends whether they remember this or that old acquaintance in the dim past. The usual sort of answer is: "Yes, wasn't she the one with the bowlegs? Wasn't he the one who was always giggling?"

Memory—the almighty despot and mainstay of our spiritual life—is the constant recipient of innumerable messages from an enormously ramified department of information, and it seems that the memory of these messages—particularly if they have any emotional significance —quickly makes notes under the heading: distinguishing features—as they do on passports and such.

Bergman goes on to say that this is probably the only method, "but it is not worth much unless the subconscious compartment contains a more or less complete dossier."

After these arguments he asserts: "The highly simplified and, in certain respects, exaggerated picture is not only a mnemonic tool—it has importance as a medium of expression, especially for the artist."

All this is in a sense a personal declaration, especially the last passage. Just as Bergman knew that he used the caricature method "on his own responsibility," he was also aware that this was in a special sense dependent on his extraordinarily good memory. It is at this point that it is appropriate to recall his long reminiscent essay on "Örebro People I Know and Örebro People Who Are Well Known."

That sketch of his childhood environment may seem to resemble the memoirs of many other writers, but it is unusual in one respect: if my count is right, it introduces seventy-nine individuals by name—an anecdote about some, a more detailed description, a distinctive feature of most, and a personal impression of almost all of them. They tumble off the page as if they had poured out of a cornucopia. In its fertile fantasy and joy of recall, the essay clarifies the immediate relationship between the world the writer *remembers* and the world he *creates*. We now realize that the great value he placed in his lecture on memory was actually determined by personal experience. In the same way that our memory of an individual may embroider an anecdote, a defect, or a mannerism and thus evolve a perhaps unreal "character," Bergman develops his characters from a dominant trait, to which he adds one detail after another from his secret "dossier" until the picture is complete in all its magnificent "validity." "Of course he [the artist] often hears that there ain't no such animal—but if he knows he has proof in his dossier, this should not disturb him."

According to Bergman, the artist has an inner sense of truth that leads him in the right direction. Even if he refuses to present evidence and proof and documentation in his "art without extenuating circumstances," like the writer who adheres to the "caricature" method, he still has an unrelenting conscience: the sternest of judges with an especially keen nose for falsification. "For the artist not least, particularly for the one burdened with a vivid imagination, uncompromising honesty is an absolute prerequisite for well-being."

In the psychological problems he presents, Bergman sometimes approaches Dostoevsky. And he is unquestionably akin to Faulkner in his view of the relationship between society and the individual. With his "caricature" technique, he seems to be indebted to an older master of the genre, Charles Dickens. We know that it was to a great extent Dickens's own childhood world and experience that recurred in his books. And Dickens also was prone to "stock epithets" or recurrent gestures and phrases, which were used to introduce the characters to the reader. For example, His Grace Roger Bernhusen in *His Grace's Last Testament* bellows insults or endearments; likewise, Innkeeper Markurell shows his "widely spaced crocodile teeth" and makes frequent use of such cryptic remarks as: "Strange but not at all peculiar. . . ." Especially in the later books, the desire to draw caricature sometimes results in a completely caricatured portrait. For example:

Vickberg untied the strings of his nightcap. With the removal of the wide bonnet, His Grace's appearance lost some of its childishness. The reddish-blue cheeks ended in a pair of large and pendulous ears, the receding brow continued imperceptibly into a bald skull. And now two small, black, piercing eyes peered out on both sides of a sharply hooked nose.

And here is a description of Markurell watching a tableau in which his newborn son has the great honor of representing the Christ Child:

> Mr. Markurell cringed as if he expected to be beaten. He tore his fringe of fox-red hair with both hands. He was chewing tobacco, he spat into his flowered handkerchief, he blew his nose, he wept. For the tableau was enchantingly beautiful and its focus was Mr. Markurell's first-born and only son.

The appearance of both men is reminiscent of figures in Bergman's childhood. They were there in his memory. As already mentioned, one of them was his own godfather, Baron Stedingk, who once upon a time had been the model for the children's game of "playing baron"; the other one was a fat, redheaded Örebro contractor, who did business with Bergman's father and who often waddled in and out of the Bergman home when Hjalmar was a child.

At the same time, neither a good memory nor colorful models are enough to produce a poet, a creator of characters. More than psychological fantasy and talent for drawing "caricatures" are required. The art of storytelling is also needed. It is not enough for a writer to see an individual and sense that person's inner drama if he or she cannot invent the situations or conflicts to reveal that drama or write down the words that will convince the reader.

But storytelling was Bergman's strong point. It could also be his weakness. Even during his last indifferent years, he could always come up with a story on demand. The story was inevitably ingenious and surprising, but it was not always interesting in the more profound sense of the word. But the desire to tell a story never left him; it was a kind of built-in reflex in his mind and heart.

During his best years his stories were drastic, seething with fantasy, pointed, and full of surprises—as befits a caricaturist. The characters are unforgettable. When Markurell entertains the examiners at lunch in the master's room (to ensure that his

son will pass his examination) and then innocently produces a
paper from his pocket to offer the school a donation, this is a
blatant attempt at bribery, an outrage, and a scandal, the "credibility" of which there is every reason to question. But the *validity*,
which it is the author's task to create, is impeccable: no hand
trembles, no eyebrow is raised; and each person in the scene
behaves exactly as one would expect, that is, according to the
roles assigned them. Every word is revealing: from the examiner,
who has totally concentrated on the delicious food, and on to
the headmaster of the school, who declines the offer but is
thinking only of the scandal and of the disastrous consequences
his refusal will have on the town and certain prominent citizens.
No reader can question the effectiveness of the episode in de-
picting Markurell as a type or, for that matter, in describing the
nature of the capitalistic society in which he lives or, finally, the
idiosyncracies of his unaffected personality. The peculiar situation and Markurell, the man, are totally interrelated. If you accept
the one, you must accept the other. The two elements support
one another and the reader's doubt is suspended. And, in Bergman's view, this is how Michelangelo depicted the creation of
Adam by God the Father in the Sistine Chapel: "The magnificent
and compelling simplicity of the gesture gave the work the
honor and the dignity of an axiom."

But the blow falls, and rich Mr. Markurell understands his
true predicament at the very moment that he believes he will
triumph. A few hours later, he lifts his safe to hurl it at his
wife—his betrayer. It is a logical action, a totally understandable
reaction. What can stop such a ruthless man? But Mrs. Markurell doesn't flinch. She defies him. Showing no fear, she insults
him unmercifully: Markurell, the self-made man who holds the
financial fate of the town in his hands; she calls him a worm and
a blind fool. How could he have been such an idiot all these
years as not to have seen how things really were and who the
father of the black-haired son was? Isn't he a flaming redhead
himself? Is there one single likeness between him and his sup-
posed offspring?

Her unexpected stand and her shocking words suddenly establish a balance between the two, and the neglected wife— "that woman I have"—immediately acquires status. The safe is thrown aside and Markurell's self-analysis begins, his biblical remorse, his attempt to understand the order of things, his railing against God.

It is obvious that a character like Markurell, who evokes such grotesquely magnificent situations and then plays the main part in them, will inevitably take on extraordinary proportions in the mind of the reader. We can never forget him.

The "vitality" or "color" or "force"—or whatever we want to call the traits that make Agnes Borck, in *Thy Rod and Thy Staff*, such a convincing character—derives from this same mastery of the narrative art. In her youth she was a calculating little creature: ruthless, determined to get on in the world. As a girl she saved her money in a piggy bank. Her father gets drunk and steals her savings. She calls for the police—a strange man has stolen my money!—but when the police officer arrives, his very presence is obviously all that is needed; no accusations are required, no confession is expected. She gets her money back and thus has triumphed over her father, but she has to leave home.

The same characteristics are illustrated so clearly and in such detail in her intrigues before her marriage to Borck, the merchant, that readers are as impressed by her infamous shrewdness as they are shocked by her indefatigable determination. She didn't lure the boss, but he was forced to take her, the modest, decent maiden who so unexpectedly found herself in compromising circumstances.

As an old woman, Grandmother sits on her bed and says her evening prayers. She does this each evening: practically the entire story is related in these nightly reports to Our Lord. Her words are a most intricate mixture of piety and primitive will power, and the old woman and her situation are revealed in the first sentences of the book:

Grandma was taking the good Lord to task. She herself believed that she was saying her evening prayers, but her tone was familiar after so many years of conversing with Him. Sometimes she was almost irreverent. She might say:

"If only for once you would do what I want."

Or:

"What did you get for that, dear God? You got fooled, that's what you got."

Or even worse:

"You can go to the dickens, the way You've been acting."

Things that one can say to husband and children but not to Our Lord. Though it is true that certain events and episodes may seem strange. And if you've been around for three-quarters of a century as Grandma has, you have the right to speak your mind on one thing and another. Particularly if the Lord has blessed you with a good head and common sense.

In this and other ways, the rich significance of events in Bergman's books is intensified by the dialogue, which is in dialect in Grandma's case. In other cases the language is more formal, more parodied, as in the book about the incompetent and pretentious Herr von Hancken, whose only claim to fame is that he invented a mouse trap.

"When I have a mishap," the humorless man complains, "everybody exclaims: 'Oh, how ridiculous!' The good Lord has denied me most of the usual advantages. I am fully aware of this. But why should He deny me the respect and sympathy of my fellow creatures. The day my neck is in a noose, everybody will laugh their heads off."

He is quite right, of course. Such is the depth of misery. Once when the impulsive and optimistic inventor Swedenhielm was dropping off to sleep on the sofa, one of his children commented:

"That's his strong point. When things get dispirited, he goes to sleep. And when he wakes up, spirits rise."

Swedenhielm himself remarked about this peculiarity of his:

"If I stop joking, I stop for good."

Comments like this may leave an impression of intensity—in this case of high spirits—which reflects on the persons to whom it refers and gives them an unusual and festive aura, even though they actually may be tragic figures.

For many prose writers, style seems to be the source from which events emerge. Style is the medium of meditation; thought and meditation create the atmosphere in which the whole story is rooted. This was not true for Hjalmar Bergman. His language exists to create and depict events; the events exist to describe characters and situations. In my opinion, at least, the atmosphere springs from situations, characters and destinies, and the language adapts itself to this variable with utter suppleness.

Detailed descriptions—independent of events or human actions—are extremely rare. There may be the occasional exception to this rule in the works of Bergman's youth and obviously in certain of his plays; apparent exceptions are his half-humorous attempts in certain of his works to create atmosphere with the help of rhymes, jingles, and, especially, proverbs.

The story of *Ma at Sutre Inn* is told to the accompaniment of this sort of poetic folk saying and figure of speech, but the proverbs are so typical of the peculiarities of the protagonist's nature and environment that they must nevertheless be regarded as tools of characterization. This close relationship between language and action (event) gives the style its firm, muscular tone.

We practically never encounter a lyrical description of a landscape, and detailed psychological analyses are almost nonexistent; external qualities are usually described briefly and often only in suggestive flashes. "I perceived it as a glance, a nod, a gesture. . . ."[4]

Presumably it was the material itself: the individual in motion, the event and its underlying psychological or symbolical import, that sparked his imagination. The ease with which he made films probably had something to do with this quality. It was easier for him than for most writers to rework his stories in very different form. He produced *His Grace's Last Testament* first as a novel, then as a film, and finally as a radio play—even though he grumbled about the difficulties involved. He turned his Markurell novel into a play that was almost equally good. In other words, he was not tied to the original form of the work: he saw it as an *event* that had meaning *in itself*.

As I shall show later in detail, this did not stop him from producing magnificent effects with the help of stylistic imitations. Here his means were extremely economical—they took up no room—but, through diction and syntax he could conjure up another era, another style than that of the twentieth century. As I have already mentioned, his first mature novels seem to have emerged from his memory. In a sense, he assumes the role of a chronicler, who either relates what he himself has seen or heard or reproduces events from old notes. This quality first appears in *We Books, Krooks and Rooths* (a chronicle of a town) and is even more pronounced in *Comedies in Bergslagen* (about an entire region and its fortunes over more than a century). Here he borrowed certain stylistic devices used by Selma Lagerlöf before him in describing an iron-mining district, or life on farms and estates. Certain strongly introverted works, like *The Loewen Stories*, are written in the first person and faintly reminiscent of Dostoevsky's *The Gambler* or Hamsun's *Hunger*.

It was not until 1919 that Bergman adopted a sprightly, conversational manner of telling his story, with interpolations and divagations and with flashes of "academic" humor, which he used quite frequently from that time on. It is the role or the point of view of the author that was now altered: he observes the course of events from a distance, almost, as it were, from the clouds. The style is apparently capricious, but in reality it serves his method of composition well in the novels after 1919. Frankly, almost omnisciently, he relates the "past" in these books in small portions and with digressions as the different phases of events succeed one another. Occasional popular Swedish novelists have related their plots in a "distant" manner; Swedish academic wit, parody, humorous pomposity, and learned stylization are favored ingredients. On occasion there is also in Bergman a link with the romantic irony of the beginning of the nineteenth century:

with E.T.A. Hoffman, for example, and with Dickens's comic exaggeration—even though Bergman's mirth often conceals abysses of tragedy and horror and only occasionally does he allow us the relief of laughter.

Like that of all his contemporaries, Hjalmar Bergman's prose is rooted in the tradition of Strindberg and in the Swedish 1890s. It possesses balance, directness, lucidity: all virtues which Strindberg pioneered; but, as already mentioned, it also includes pastiche and stylization. His most original contribution to this tradition is his habit of providing information in extremely concentrated form, his rapid transitions from one mood to another. An example may be cited from *Ljung, Medardus and I.* When the youth Medardus indignantly denies his comrades' sniggering accusations that he is courting their adored Hannele (the little actress who is mortally ill at the end of the book), he replies:

"Idiots! The girl belongs to the company. I might as well kiss my own sister—if I had a sister."
He made us feel quite deflated. We took our revenge by laughing at him. He who laughs last laughs best.
My sweet Hannele, finally you laughed.
No one laughs finally.

The mood changes in each of the last three sentences. It is constantly shifting. Permit me a brief comparison with a dramatic work. Joe Meng, in the comedy *The Rabble*, delivers a bitter attack on the stupid people who are taunting the "fantast" (they want to drown him in his own "slimy spittle"), but suddenly he has a change of heart—and then still another:

"He has ennobled even your stupid mocking grins. But why mock? One day his heart will wither between his fleshless ribs, just as yours will."
Short pause.
"Oh, grandmother, if you only knew the plans I am toying with!"

It should be noted that the pause is explicitly designated as short. These "short pauses" influence the style in practically all Bergman's works; they give it some of its special quality.

The facility for stylization and the bantering tone that are seldom absent are related to a taste for outright pastiche.

Bergman reached that effect with a minimum of word changes. *Herr von Hancken* seems to have come from early nineteenth century Sweden. The Bergslagen story, *The Dance at Frötjärn*, now and again resembles *A Thousand and One Nights*. The novel *Solivro* recalls a medieval tale.

It is important at this point to remember that an unusual character's way of speaking or thinking (for example, in *Thy Rod and Thy Staff*) can also be regarded as a kind of pastiche. It is a matter of making the style as a whole into an integral part of the fable, a support for the fiction; the style is a part of the conception of the work. Bergman seldom writes impressionistically and directly, as if he had just encountered the person he is telling us about. Impressions have always been worked over in his memory and fantasy by the time they are presented, and that which is impressionistic has been eliminated.

This method can be called a *fictive attitude* through which the story is filtered. It gives the impression that the writer personally is vastly amused, is *playing*. (Perhaps this is what stands in the way of the impressionistic, direct effect.) A strong element of *make-believe* also is part of the attitude. The author pretends to be indignant, describing his young characters' outbursts of rage with pretended sympathy, their folly with a melancholy pretense of distress—here we have an ingenious and good-natured raillery with people's weaknesses and shortsightedness, which often masks a certain softness. All this is obviously reflected in the language which sometimes surges forth in long, absurdly pompous passages or sometimes consists of short exclamations, a sentence broken down into its component parts: "The Lord! Be! Thanked!" or the like.

It is this raillery, these glances aside, these lightning-fast, ironical glimpses, ever present even in tragic situations, that so often seem to make Hjalmar Bergman's books sparkle—not with a light, summery sparkle, but rather, with the glitter of jet or a moonlit lake.

Hjalmar Bergman's storytelling often focuses upon grand intentions followed by ignominious outcomes. The effect is sometimes humorous, as when a character tries to drown himself in a brook but finds the water too shallow. It can also be tragic, as when Markurell discovers that his whole life is built on the illusion of his fatherhood. It can be heartrending and hopeless, as when the clown finds that his daughter is so eccentric that their community of spirit will remain a dream.

The road to such discoveries is usually long, tortuous, and full of surprises. Sometimes it is a matter of an overt interplay of wills, when the wills cross one another; here the course of events is followed from the outside. Other times the drama is observed from within by the actors, and it then resembles a nightmare with the compulsive evolution of a dream.

Whether the protagonist is an outsider or a typical character of will, events are always set into motion by a single strong act of will. Markurell's plan for his son's future was clear soon after the story began. But Leonard Loewen, the outsider, also takes on a project: namely, to break down the class barriers in the house in which he lives. Both men experience the inevitable disappointment: the world is far from what they had believed. Grandmother and Herr von Hancken are equally good examples. The strong personalities, or those who believe themselves to be strong, run things according to their own short-sighted will and on the basis of their own experience. All is well for some time. But since no one completely controls reality or understands its laws and—above all—since no one can help seeing the world in the light of his or her own desires, the final outcome is usually disastrous.

Sometimes, however, the main theme is not an act of a single will. *His Grace's Last Testament* consists of a battle between two wills, the baron's and his sister's. The baron has his own ideas about his testament, and his sister has hers: here we have the conflict. But the outcome is determined by a third force: the whims of young Blenda. In *St. Canute's Fair* and *Ma at Sutre Inn*, a tangled skein of wills, either at odds with or independent of one another, gradually develops. The former book thus comes to resemble an old-fashioned tale of action, in which financial coups and even murders are secretly plotted and in which an underhanded threat by one character is repaid in kind by another. Finally chance steps in and decides the outcome. Since the emphasis in this book is on an image of the environment, no one of the characters holds the limelight longer than another.

This is even more true of *We Books, Krooks and Rooths,* which is a sort of collective portrait; the action covers the history of more than a century. The world changes and the town with it: powerful planners disappear in the mainstreams of the chronicle; they appear to be alert and active, but there is little they can do to determine the course of events. At the end of the book, when we get to the social reform project, wills are tugging in every direction: clear-sighted wills, shortsighted wills, and purely eccentric wills which have never grasped the basic objectives. When all these component forces intermingle, the outcome differs totally from what any individual could have anticipated—the resultant in this power parallelogram points in the direction of absurdity, and life becomes a muddle, even though all the characters have had some sort of sensible motive for their actions.

Ma at Sutre Inn, on the other hand, is completely dominated by a single character: a woman, the mistress of the house. Her authoritative desire to manage life wisely and well for her children and grandchildren seems to determine the line of action. But she and her family unwittingly run into life's "tornado," as Bergman sees it—a struggle between impulses, some of which cannot be anticipated—and no one will give in. Her son, the innkeeper, is one factor in the power game; the dissolute Count Arnfelt and his appetites another; the fermenting discontent of the Count's workers a third; the favorite son's love for the daughter of the itinerant peddler a fourth. Ma herself turns out to have several wills, including a secret one of which she is unaware. Plans are disrupted; death and disaster befall Sutre. And with tragedy comes acceptance. This is a tale of hubris.[5]

Bergman often excels in his ability to shift a situation so as to disclose a new and unexpected facet of the story. These maneuvers reveal a sense of power, a command not only of the course of events but of the reader as well. Even as a child, he frightened his sisters with his horror stories, fascinated his playmates with his understanding of the "devil's will." In his lecture, "Caricature and Cliché," Bergman himself speaks of Balzac in terms that are illustrative in this connection: he admires the *sense of power* of this great creator of tragic figures. Certainly it is truth that Balzac tells, but it is "truth by the grace of Balzac." Here we encounter another aspect of the concept of the artist's compelling gesture. One might say that it also reveals something of the born storyteller's attitude to falsehood.

For Bergman also presents other examples that throw light on his ideal. He tells of a mild Quaker who, in a group of raconteurs, reveals himself to be the greatest liar of them all—"one of those who know how to lie about facts, thanks to that faculty for combination that is usually the prerogative of our politicians." The Quaker's story is told in interesting terms. It was "incredibly thrilling and incredibly incredible, but put together with such brilliant simplicity that the audience was completely captivated by the magic power of the lie."

Hjalmar Bergman took genuine delight in the actual process of lying, which may be a primitive and, for that reason, refreshing quality in refined literary products.

A good lie has a magic power of aesthetic quality; pure fabrication without ulterior motives may have an aesthetic value. This appears to be Bergman's view in free association to Oscar Wilde, and it would be foolish to try to challenge him on this point. It is unquestionably fatal when art reproduces reality with such fidelity that we are unaware of the "lie" of fantasy, of its duplicity, its determination not to be enslaved by reality.

But the interplay between falsehood and truth in art must obey certain laws. The naked, fictitious event does not become art simply because it resembles the ordinary, banal, and credible; it must have secret under- and overtones. Nor will it succeed merely by being incredible and grotesque. But one way in which it can achieve an artistic effect is by imitating life's own special incredibility at the same time that it gives us a wink to let us know that it is dressed up, disguised, actually an invention.

In real life, a particular event may possibly occur once and never be repeated: thus there are events that the average liar cannot possibly invent. As we know, reality is and must be just a little more wonderful than fiction. To quote Bergman, "a liar of the first water" is another matter. He recounts the unique event so unabashedly that the very incredibility and brilliant simplicity of the anecdote's construction become the criterion for truth. The story becomes "valid," like Michelangelo's Creation. Our critical sense is aware that a lie is a lie, perhaps even a blatant lie—excellent! Because if the illusion is overdone, it cancels its own effect, as in the theater. The critic, simultaneously, gains a sense of artistic well-being at the straightforward "naturalness" of the composition, the presentation of the lie.

Thus is dignity conferred on naked fabrication. This is a part of Hjalmar Bergman's art. He cultivates it in many contexts, but never with such consummate skill as in his pastiches, in which the tone of a chronicle or an ancient document gives an extra accent of credibility to the sensational and almost unbelievable happenings. That is why we must turn to *Comedies in Bergslagen*, particularly Part One, and to *Herr von Hancken* to find this aesthetic of untruth, its astonishing charm, exemplified in abundance. But samples of it are present in many of Bergman's works. Often it is a slight dash of extravagant, well-placed falsehood, a surprising piece of information offered in passing (in an especially calm and credible tone of voice—as if the matter were of no significance) that gives a story the special Bergman flavor. Gulliver's author had this gift, and so had Robinson Crusoe's.

However, what is revealed by the various situations in the story, what is squeezed forth like a precious drop, is almost always a human destiny, an individual. But the individual and the disappointments and surprises encountered nevertheless conceal something else again: a problem, an insight, a paradoxical truth.

As an example, and to conclude this chapter on the storyteller, I would choose one of the works in which the fabrication may seem exceptionally spontaneous and dreamlike in direction and intent: namely, the first volume of *Comedies in Bergslagen*. As I already mentioned, the title of this book is *Two Families*, and the first story describes, in chronicle fashion, the origin of the conflict between the Klockeberga family called Siedel and the Ryglinge family—in which the names of the peasants alternate between Erik Janse (son of Jan) and Jan Erse (son of Erik). The episodes succeed one another as in a dream, but the dream has different levels, some of greater significance than others.

An exceedingly tense episode is the one mentioned earlier in which Bailiff Jan Erse—drinking and boasting among a group of friends—carries out his threat to beat his son till his cane breaks. His normal practice, under these circumstances, is to prepare the cane in advance, cutting a deep score into it so that it will break easily, thus awing spectators by his seeming brutality. This time, befuddled with drink, he forgets to cut into the cane beforehand. As a result, he maims his son for life, physically and mentally. The father, too, is a changed man from that night on, and we can now read him like a book—although before he was almost unknown to us.

This episode is one among many. Bigmouthed, jovial individuals often behave in this fashion: they generate misfortune. But it also resembles several other episodes in which a despotic father tortures a beloved son, physically or mentally. Two Bergmanian motifs meet in these stories. First, the dangerous progression of a strong will, the risks of naïve self-assertion. Second, the father-despot. The seemingly dreamlike aimlessness has its aim after all; it is by no means insignificant or produced merely for the pleasure of fabrication.

The foregoing events occur in the story "Klockeberga and Ryglinge." In the next story, "Madame Beata, Jan Erse and the Mine Manager," the action develops over years and decades, and new generations of Siedels and Janses (Erses) continue to inflict grave injustices upon one another. Guilt and enmity grow ever deeper. The youngest Jan Erse, a farmhand under old Madame Beata Siedel, broods on revenge on her powerful family, from the time of his sixteenth birthday. A knife will be his weapon. Finally it seems that Madame Beata's grandson, the massively built manager Jörgen Siedel, is within his reach. He plans to stab him with his own hand.

Before the story reached this point, unfortunate occurrences had already struck Ryglinge, events that seem meaningless and dreadful when they happen. The hectic pace of these events now slows down, the style grows taut, light is focused on the lonely journey of the manager and Jan Erse through Bergslagen. In Jan Erse's eyes, Jörgen Siedel becomes a powerful and competent man, whose counsel is sought by crowds of Bergslagen inhabitants. He is also a brave man, as he was the one to suggest this expedition alone with his mortal enemy. The young man has never seen him like this before. Moreover, Jan Erse is astonished to learn that Siedel's womanizing stems from a secret, well-hidden disappointment in love when the man was young. This is the sorrow that has plagued the powerful Jörgen Siedel all his adult life. Finally: he is ill, mortally ill: an old wound, which Jan Erse himself had inflicted upon him in the past, has reopened and is now festering. Siedel is in a bad way: he deserves sympathy; Jan Erse postpones his plan. But once again Jörgen Siedel shows his bad side, during an attack of fever, and Jan Erse's hatred is refueled. These postponed decisions and renewed convictions constantly revive the tension in the story.

Toward the end of the trip, the two companions are forced to seek refuge from wolves by hiding in a sheepfold, and there Jörgen Siedel's condition grows rapidly worse. The powerful, dying man, magnificent in his way—generous and brave but also debauched, ruthless and responsible for the unhappiness of many people—haltingly recites his last Lord's Prayer, and Jan Erse is so bitterly ashamed that he cannot help his mortal enemy to remember the words. Desperately Jan tries to bring himself to the point that he can carry out his intention. But now the wolves attack over the roof, which collapses. The long, bitter, spiteful feud between the families comes to an end when the irreconcilable avenger Jan Erse, young and strong as he is, refuses to desert his dead enemy. Standing over the corpse, he defends it in blind rage. When Erse is finally found, his body has been ripped to pieces by the wolves, but Jörgen Siedel's body is unharmed.

CHAPTER 12

The Dramatist

NEXT to Strindberg, Hjalmar Bergman is Sweden's most important and popular dramatist. In Bergman's youth, Strindberg's name may have been controversial, but it was nonetheless the greatest in Swedish letters. Inevitably, Bergman was influenced in style and theme by this giant who was thirty-four years his senior.

When Bergman was a child, Strindberg was considered the great dissenter in Swedish literature, a radical naturalist. He never met him in person. Strindberg's voice was silent during the 1890s, but he underwent his conversion during the young writer's impressionable years. After his long silence he came back with a completely new style, in a completely new spirit. The style was symbolic, occasionally dreamlike, and the old master became an inspiration for later modernistic currents in European literature, including expressionism and even absurd theater.

The new approaches to drama that Strindberg created were therefore available to his younger colleague from the very beginning. He was in a position, it would seem, to feel free in his choice of style and technique, free at least from naturalistic conventions, and he could gradually feel his way toward his own personal dramatic form.

In reality, an act of liberation, such as Strindberg accomplished with his dream plays, is not necessarily understood properly by succeeding generations. The younger writers do not grasp the liberating nature of the new approach; they experience it as just another style to be followed or rejected. Hjalmar Bergman began by following it, but soon went his own way.

In a letter to his friend Ellen Key, the twenty-one-year-old Bergman wrote:

I have been the admirer of many, not least Nietzsche; but I've been apprenticed to no one, least of all to Nietzsche. Shakespeare was my first great acquaintance, then Strindberg. One doesn't make such acquaintances without certain losses. You have mentioned one.

(Ellen Key's letters to Hjalmar Bergman have been lost, but obviously she had mentioned a certain dependance on Strindberg in the play she had been asked to read, *Mary, Mother of Jesus.*)

At this juncture, however, Bergman had at least two unpublished dramatic efforts behind him. The oldest extant is a Christian penitential drama entitled *Strid* (*Struggle*). It was probably written before he was twenty. Here the Strindbergian influence is clear. It is an immature piece, interesting for its vigorous presentation of a moral problem. Humility and contrition, here, provide the only road to peace of mind. Characteristic of Hjalmar Bergman is the contrast between the innocent, bright idealism of the two young men and the negativism of the defiant, penitent Albert in his attempt to explain to them that the world is evil, that the freedom they are awaiting is an illusion, that "every thought is fettered," that "every action rattles with chains."

Harald, one of the youths, replies:

"The world is not evil for him who has done no evil. The world shall be our battlefield. There we shall fight for good. We shall search every corner, and we shall deal mortal blows to evil wherever we find it. Pure it shall be, our world!"

These naïvely idealistic words are echoed twenty years later in the play, *The Portal.*

Förrädare (*Traitors*), an actable play presumably written in 1904, also shows Strindbergian influences and contains one or two comic Shakespearean episodes. It deals with pacifism: an officer helps an enemy to escape and misfortune later befalls them both. The play expresses an ethic of compassion and gives a picture of the external impotence of good will. *Mary, Mother of Jesus* (1905) contrasts beautifully with these two apprentice works. It makes interesting reading, has a lyrical effect in many passages, and depicts the characters in simple terms. But it is a closet drama—or actable only after thorough revision. It has been performed on one occasion only in a greatly abridged version in an avant-garde theater.

Here the technical prototype was not a modern dramatist but the Passion Play at Oberammergau, which the young Hjalmar Bergman had seen in 1901. *Mary, Mother of Jesus* might well be called a passion drama and, like the famous Bavarian play, it is divided into sections plus a prologue and epilogue. It describes the relationship of Jesus to His family and His disciples; it shows how death and crucifixion finally are inevitable. The theme of the play is twofold: a strongly emotional involvement in Jesus of Nazareth (who is depicted as a man and a prophet, not as the Son of God) and a profound interest in the strong-willed being who defied a world: Mary. She is the first in Bergman's long series of strong and important women, of mothers.

Mary, Mother of Jesus was promising, particularly in a few highly dramatic situations. For example, when Mary herself screams with the others: "Crucify Him!" She does this for purely personal reasons, which at that point are known to the reader-viewer; but her action is shocking nevertheless. The play is ingeniously planned, and the scenes are so skillfully presented that they bring out Jesus' gentleness and sublime destiny in violent contrast to the varying expectations and pressures of the people around Him. But the play can scarcely be regarded to be of interest from the strictly theatrical point of view; it was relatively unplayable at the time of publication, due to its length and to the constantly changing scenes—perhaps also because of the length of the speeches. The idea was more interesting than the form. The fantasy at work in the play knew no limits, but it refused—perhaps for that very reason—to concern itself with practical problems of the theater.

It was neither Shakespeare nor Strindberg but Ibsen who came to influence Hjalmar Bergman in his next years as a playwright. Even *Mary, Mother of Jesus* had a trace of Ibsen: namely, in the relationship between mother and son, in which the attentive reader can discern certain similarities with *Fru Inger till Östråt* (*The Lady of Östråt*). During these early years, however, Hjalmar Bergman was introduced into the Lindberg family, famous in theatrical circles—a member of the family later became his wife. August Lindberg was an actor, a director, and a prominent monologist; he had gained fame as the foremost interpreter of Ibsen in the Nordic countries and at one time had his own touring company, playing *Ghosts* and other dramas by the great Norwegian.[1] He was an impulsive and eloquent man, full of enthusiasm, and he could talk endlessly about Ibsen. It was natural that the twenty-year-old Hjalmar Bergman came to see technical problems, at least, from Ibsen's viewpoint. Consequently, Bergman's next play, *The Purity of the Family*, presented a violent contrast to the idealistic biblical drama of 1905. This new play was a harshly revealing drama about pure humbug in family life, about the ability of the idealistic lie to give rise to misfortune. The effect is almost terrifying, and no director ever dared to produce the play.

The personal experiences that may have generated this vitriolic play are not known; but the literary impulse derived from Ibsen at the time he was preoccupied with the unmasking of lies and nonsense. A weak idealist renounces a scientific career to wed the sensual Lina; he has found happiness in the name of "purity," but purity is here an illusion. His wife betrays him with a friend of the family, and his daughter, Agda, is seduced by the son of her father's employer—with her mother's blessing. The laxity of her home has poisoned Agda. The whole situation is clarified during a family party to celebrate the fiftieth birthday of the unfortunate father (who works as a cashier). A

hereditary motif *à la Ghosts* is included in the play; one of the
hereditary traits is hideous, sniggering laughter—a demented
laugh marks the end of the play. All that remains for the character who has never seen through his illusions is the reflex of
laughter, mocking laughter.

However, this caustic directness, this open aggressiveness was
not very well suited to Hjalmar Bergman's imaginative nature.
Soon we find him deeply involved in another dramatist who conquered Europe at the turn of the century: Maeterlinck (1862–
1949). Here a new kind of symbolism—the French variety—was
being introduced to the young by the Belgian poet; not even
Strindberg escaped his influence. The Belgian worked in the
spirit of the fairy tale play in a stylized nonmodern environment
with hesitant, fragile, nostalgic moods expressed by hints, pauses,
the repetition of simple, poetic phrases. In 1907, Hjalmar Bergman published two short Maeterlinckian dialogues as sort of
trial pieces. In *Fru Wendlas kedja* (*Lady Wendla's Chain*),
which had a historical setting, he tried to apply what he had
learned, but he did not entirely succeed. The mixture of styles
is irritating, and certain elements of tragic fate are more confusing than effective. The symbolic gold chain referred to in the
title is an Ibsenian object, but it is fraught with a belief in fate
that was foreign to Ibsen. At the same time, the play had several actable scenes—concerned with fire, firelight, terror, and
frightening memories—and it had the honor of representing the
young generation of writers when the Royal Dramatic Theater
re-opened in Stockholm in 1908.

An old Norse play, *Det underbara leendet* (*The Wonderful
Smile*), is formally more satisfying but also more overtly dependent on Maeterlinck. Here Bergman tries to combine the influence of his new master with that of the Edda. Vague allusions,
hesitant, melancholy dialogue, words of undefined fear and other
obscure passions blend with occasionally harsh notes reminiscent
of the Icelandic saga; the mixture sometimes makes an odd impression. The theme is the Vaulund saga: a triangle drama involving the imprisoned master smith, his former wife Alvit, and

King Nidad's daughter Böthvild. The most personal ingredient in the play is the mysterious Alvit and the marvelous smile that symbolizes her infinite submissiveness: "You are my beloved. From you I willingly take life and death." This total feminine submissiveness embodies, in strongly secret and congealed form, Hjalmar Bergman's rather strange ideal of love; it is in accord with the jealousy that plagued him all his life. It was this dream, his personal saga, that he was to renounce in *Sagan* (*The Legend*), a play written in the 1920s.

Maeterlinck, however, was an obsession only of his early youth. Bergman soon wrote a couple of comedies and farces in a completely different and relatively uncontrived style; none of these efforts were accepted by any theater. In 1912, he returned with a serious and skillfully constructed play, more mature than anything he had done previously. It was called *Lönngången* (*The Secret Passage*). The undiscovered secret passage in the middle of an old house—in which the owner had committed a crime many years ago—is a rather clear, but not actually obtrusive, Ibsenian symbol. Bergman is a disciple of Ibsen, but now an independent one.

The play is so constructed that its contents consist of information about past events. The tension is related to what has already happened. Thus, the play ends when the past has been clarified. But this action-fraught information is provided in a simple, highly dramatic manner, and the characters stand out in clear relief. The play's weakness is the protagonist: Mr. Suneson, manager of the Forssa mineworks, has much to conceal—he has a secret passage in his house—but he remains a psychological mystery. As a result, there is a risk of the interest being concentrated on the crime motif, as in a thriller. His wife, on the other hand, is more exciting, more subtly depicted. In a state of desperation, she has retired to a room at the top of the house, from which she observes what is going on in the garden.

The situation in the play seems natural, in no sense contrived: the distance, the lack of communication between man and wife

are brought out clearly and evocatively. The fact that the play
was never performed was not due to technical flaws; producers
were simply put off by the unadulterated tragedy of its theme.

At about the same time, Bergman was working on a play
which was to be a great success when it was finally staged in
1915: *Parisina*. Although this, too, is a tragedy, it is also a colorful love story reminiscent of *Tristan and Isolde* or *Romeo and
Juliet*. Bergman was not unaware of the resemblance to the
Tristan legend: he himself refers to it in the text. Information
about the past is relatively unimportant, and the emphasis is
on the question of what will happen when the young couple's
love is discovered. The young woman is Parisina, wife of the
old Marquis Niccolò d'Este in Ferrara. Her lover is Ugo, the
Marquis's own son.

Here the portrayal of the environment bears slight traces of
both Shakespeare and Strindberg, but on the whole it is pure
Bergman: inventive and assured in its dramatic construction.
The plot contains both a description of life in gay Ferrara and
a subplot among the courtiers. The sympathies of the author and
the reader are fixed hypnotically on the two lovers.

But the violent increase in tension in the last act derives from
Niccolò and his inner struggle; he is cruel and proud and venge-
ful by nature, but he loves his son—and now he is searching for
the truth. Nevertheless, the well-constructed drama reverts at
the end to the Tristan-and-Isolde romance of the two young
people: "Parisina—is death not a release?" Ugo asks, and in the
last lines of the play he rejoices: "God has released us."

It is clear that until 1915, his thirty-second year, Hjalmar
Bergman was experimenting with different styles, not aimlessly
but with a degree of consistency. The explanation has been given
in the biographical chapter: he wanted his plays to be produced,
and the opportunities for young playwrights were rare in
Sweden in those days.

In 1915, encouraged by the success of *Parisina*, he set off in
a direction that was purely his own. This approach also met

with obstacles, but it did lead to one or two truly memorable, genuinely effective, and moving plays.

He was no longer searching for moods through language, as in the Maeterlinckian plays; he did not lean on the picturesque or on historical settings as in *Parisina*; nor did he attempt to divulge the past gradually, as in the plays influenced by Ibsen. The plots evolved primarily on the stage before the eyes of the audience—the concentration of action on stage was the purpose and secret of the plays; overtones and poetic associations were there, but they grew out of the events and were tied to visible accessories.

A glance at the scenic arrangements in the three "marionette plays" is illustrative.

In *Death's Harlequin* (which is based on his memories of the death of his father) a powerful old shipbuilder is lying on his deathbed in a room backstage. The significance of everything that is said and done by the actors is intensified by the knowledge of what is happening in the invisible room.

In *Mr. Sleeman Is Coming*, the best of the plays, all the action takes place in the home of two old women, where time seems to stand still. The passage of time in this narrow world is marked by a tall grandfather clock: its ticking marks the approach of doom.

A *Shadow* is played in a pavilion at night, in moonlight, and in the light of dawn. Shadows glide up to the wall and turn into people; other people approach and converge to investigate the cause of the shadows.

The characters' past lives are of no particular importance in these plays (with the exception of *Death's Harlequin*); earlier events are merely intimated; that which happens nevertheless seems to be inevitable. This lack of biographical information about the characters probably explains why the author called the three *Marionette Plays*.

As Consul Broman in *Death's Harlequin* lies dying behind closed doors, life goes on before the eyes of the audience. All characters are delineated, sometimes even unmasked, through their attitudes toward death and the old man. The children's lines reveal attitudes ranging from love and respect to a suppressed, repressed, thus hatelike love. The scale mounts to rancor and rebelliousness, particularly in Bertil; broken by his father's will, he vainly tries to prove that he is capable of assuming his father's role and wants to do it.

A veiled, unknown, and unnamed woman arrives on the scene. Consul Broman has summoned her to his bedside. She is the woman he has loved and betrayed. This is all we are told. While friends and enemies are transacting business in his office, it gradually becomes clear that the position of Tofta Shipyards is completely undermined; meanwhile the woman and the dying man speak of their memories, and a photograph of Broman is produced from a drawer. At the end of the play, the still unnamed woman returns to the stage; she presses the photograph to her face. Her last words to the whispering, intriguing men: "And now, gentlemen, you may raise your voices." In other words: He is dead; you need no longer be afraid.

Here Bergman analyzes the role and significance of a "great" personality, the workings and meaning of so-called authority: the town may flourish for the time being, but everyone must dance to the master's tune. In the words of the doctor in the play, the "death doctor," they become marionettes. It seems that God entrusts the reins only to a select few in the world. Only a few rule—only one in Tofta. This obviously entails certain disadvantages: servility, hypocrisy, irresponsibility in those who allow themselves to be ruled. And some are crushed. But the force of the ruler, the measure of his personality, his ability to inspire respect, even a kind of love, are disclosed at his death— if not before.

The background, the town of Tofta, is represented by the banker, who coldly takes note of the financial situation; the vicar, who awaits a donation to the church; the head engineer, who is prepared to take a job with a rival company; the crude sheriff; and Mr. Jonsson, the school superintendent, who is worrying about money. Things look grim: Tofta Shipyard is in bad shape. For a time, the desire to gossip unites opponents from different groups, but no one is disposed to help the consul or the company he has built. On the contrary, all are eager to pull their own chestnuts out of the fire.

In *Death's Harlequin*, the father-son motif is mingled with Bergman's romantic love theme, and the figure of the despot in all his conceit, severity, and arrogance thereby becomes apotheosized. But an echo remains—until the very last scene—of a series of sadly characteristic remarks about Broman: "Great personalities should be forbidden in small communities...."—"Love? He? He has never loved.... We always knew that he gave out of pride, not out of love...."—It is this basically well-founded evaluation of the old man that ultimately proves to be wrong. Alexander Broman had indeed loved. But his deliberate smothering of all that was youthfully genuine and tender in his nature made him what he eventually became: Alexander Broman.

The members of this big, powerful man's family, a son and two daughters, are equally complex. The son is the least interesting: his fear and incompetence are revealed repeatedly in the play. Magda, one of the daughters, is the most intriguing of the three. Brusque, strong-willed, and practical, she is attached to Tofta and to her father, whom she believes she hates. When she is summoned to her father toward the end of the play by the words, "Your father is longing for you," she rushes into the sickroom with a cry "half of triumph and half of pain": "Father longs for me! Beloved—beloved—beloved." An element of passion has been concealed in the relationship between father and daughter.

Tyra, the other daughter, is superficial, gay, and flirtatious: "Father likes me to be happy." She can't stand the oppressive atmosphere of the sickroom, but organizes a sleighride with torches in honor of the great Alexander Broman. "Unfeeling— therefore friendly to all." Together with Dr. Brising, the company physician, she comes to represent a part of the symbolic motif of the play, Harlequin's bells. For the doctor describes a marionette performance he has seen in Paris, in which Death is preceded by a Harlequin who jingles his bells. Death lost its power with the sound of the bells, and friends and enemies began to dance so that both Death and its victim were forgotten.

An ingenious touch in the play is the bell hanging on the door of the office. Each caller—and business friends are constantly dropping in—makes the bell jingle. But the horses drawing the sleigh also wear bells—their jingling is an accompaniment to the action on the stage. Terrified, all escape to their immediate concerns and, as death approaches, they carry on in their usual roles, a trivial comedy. This was probably the effect that the author intended to achieve. That it can actually be attained, on television at least, was proved by a broadcast in 1962. But the component parts of the play are difficult to weld into a single unit. The realistic ingredients compete with the symbolical; the Harlequin motif becomes subsidiary.

But *Death's Harlequin* was a fine precursor of what was to come. In January 1916, Bergman wrote the one-act play *Mr. Sleeman Is Coming*, a small dramatic masterpiece, an extremely effective symbolical story and one of the Bergman plays that is produced over and over.

The death involved here is not physical death but the death of the spirit. As Bergman himself later suggested, Mr. Sleeman is not a symbol of death but of *time*. The play is rooted in Bergman's personal, often reiterated reflections on life—its vigorous and its rigidified forms—and in his experience of the fundamental tragedy: how living beings turn into robots, life into a grimace.

The same motif appears in *Death's Harlequin*. But in that play a psychological explanation is given for the mechanical gestures: namely, fear. In *Mr. Sleeman . . .*, on the other hand, rigidity is both a symbol and a fearful vision.

The play is well thought out in scenic terms, and Bergman showed great ingenuity in devising the contrasts on which the effect of the piece depends.

Two elderly, unmarried, nineteenth century women, Mina and Bina, are the driving forces of the plot—unless they can be said to be driven by their poverty and their concepts of decency.

Anne-Marie, their niece, has been put into their care. She is a
normal young girl—pretty, graceful, and full of life. She is also
vulnerable, as she was born out of wedlock to a third sister, now
dead, whose fate as an unwed mother is evoked as an omni-
present spectre: May Anne-Marie not turn out like her mother!
Anne-Marie is now to be sacrificed in order to be supported. Her
aunts intend to deliver her into marriage to stuffy, bureaucratic,
old Mr. Sleeman (who "walks like an ataxic," according to the
stage directions), a civil servant and doer of good deeds. The
match, of course, will also relieve the financial burden of the
two aunts.

Here, youth and love are sacrificed to old age and rigidity
on the altar of parsimony and possessiveness. The opposite extreme is represented by a young hunter, clad in green, who
persuades Anne-Marie to run off with him for one last tryst in
the forest—the night before her meeting with Mr. Sleeman. . . .

This simple motif—none of the characters need to be plumbed
psychologically and each one is a prototype—obviously deserves
the epithet "marionette play." The problem resembles the one
with which Pirandello was struggling at about the same time.
In its very simplicity (which is never arid, much less "absurd"),
the play nevertheless points in the direction of the "absurd"
drama that was later to follow. The characters play to each other
according to a pattern that might be called eternal.

The basic theme and the scenic effect seem identical in this
play. The effect depends on a skillful use of scenically rewarding
media: costumes, gestures, dances, the girl's practicing of a
curtsy to greet old Mr. Sleeman, but also the ticking and striking
of the clock—which indicates that time is flying inexorably
toward the hour of Mr. Sleeman's arrival. At the beginning of
the play, before we have become aware of Mina's and Bina's
unwitting cruelty, the furniture is concealed by blue and white
dust covers. When the story reaches its climax, their dingy old
furniture, nondescript and ornate, is revealed in all its hideous
nudity.

When the play opens Anne-Marie is unaware of the "happi-

ness" and "honor" to be bestowed on her. The reading aloud
of a letter suffices to characterize both the writer (Mr. Sleeman),
the reader (Aunt Bina), and the two listeners (Mina and Anne-
Marie). Eight o'clock the following morning is the hour set for
Mr. Sleeman's arrival; when the clock strikes eight the evening
before, Anne-Marie rushes up in terror. Only twelve hours remain. She must practice her curtsy and her words of greeting.

She is then locked into her room; no one could dream that the
young hunter would be able to take her out through the window.
When he arrives, he seizes the opportunity to stop the terrible
clock and then speaks the words of love that Anne-Marie has
been longing to hear. Jubilant and terrified, she goes with him
into the forest. The only sign of what has happened is a feather
from the young man's cap lying on the old women's carpet.

When Mr. Sleeman arrives the next morning on the stroke of
eight, he is faced with a *fait accompli*: he has been deceived.
But the sacrifice is made anyway and is, in a sense, confirmed at
the moment when the "ataxic" Mr. Sleeman—with his hunchback
and his mechanical trembling voice—utters the very same words
of love that had sounded so fresh and vigorous a few hours ago
when spoken by the young hunter. Anne-Marie, too, repeats herself when she says: "If I begin to cry, I shall never be able to
stop." She bursts into tears, which elicits the final, crushingly
ironic rejoinder from Mr. Sleeman, who cheerfully says: "Happiness has its tears too."

Bergman was often concerned with the theme of change and
the process of petrification. But this time he gives it new dimen-
sions, many new directions, thanks to an almost schematic simplification. He demonstrated the full range of the idea in a film
script of the play in 1919, in which Mr. Sleeman's wait is much
longer and involves a number of different variations on the
theme: this version also comprises Anne-Marie's and the hunter's
transformation and tragedy. Here, too, the game goes to Mr.
Sleeman, as in the play.

No, it is not of old age that Bergman writes, but of change as

such, of time and the disillusion it brings, of time's murder of
all illusions of permanent happiness.

When *Marionette Plays* was published in 1917, the book included the previously mentioned one-acter entitled *En skugga*
(*A Shadow*) in addition to *Death's Harlequin* and *Mr. Sleeman
Is Coming*. *A Shadow* was performed (together with *Death's
Harlequin*) at the Royal Dramatic Theater in the spring of
1917, the occasion of the abysmal fiasco that almost finished
Bergman once and for all. The play was written in 1916, more
or less to order. The theater management wanted a one-acter
as a "filler," presumably because it found *Death's Harlequin*
too short for a full evening's entertainment.

The fact that the play was commissioned as a necessary complement and contrast to *Death's Harlequin* may explain the
author's eagerness to create appealing poetic effects. In any
case, *A Shadow* is a lyrical play about shadows and the concept
of shadows. The effect of light in the darkness of night and of
the gradual shift from early dawn to morning light is skillfully
exploited.

A Shadow also works on a symbolic level, due less to the
logical sequence of events than to romantic associations. Like
Mr. Sleeman Is Coming, this play contains the jealousy motif:
here, too, a young girl is to be sacrificed to a rich, ailing, aged
bridegroom whose jealousy is painted in broad, ruthless strokes.
Most of the action takes place the night before the wedding.
Again the bridegroom is cheated of his prey, but this time love
wins out—with the help of death. Love triumphs in its truly
romantic guise of idealism. The force that is *"fort comme la
mort"* is so pure and lofty that it demands a divorce from the
"baser self."

The shadowy atmosphere in the play is heightened by the
fact that the characters, though active on the stage, are known as
"the bridegroom," "the mother," "the manservant," etc. The
bride has a name (Vera), and so does the young man with the
stormy past (Erik), who comes to abduct her on the eve of her
wedding and who stays in her chamber while "the manservant"

stands on guard outside the door. The manservant is a comrade of Erik's from his old days of adventure; he is a rascal and a thief: Erik's baser self, one might say. The two men remind us of characters in a picaresque novel.

The action takes place in the bride's pavilion while the light is changing from moonlit dark to early morning sunshine. The bridegroom shuffles about the room with the mother looking for traces of the "shadow" he has seen from his window. It is in this room that Erik and Vera meet to plan their flight, and here that Erik and the "manservant" have their final showdown. Here the tragic climax takes place, and the groom's gift to the bride, a collection of valuable jewelry, is displayed on a table; the crucial question is whether the impoverished abducter Erik, true to his adventurous nature, will steal the jewels or leave them be, guided by his love and trust of an innocent girl. He overcomes the temptation, but the disappointed and bitter manservant steals them instead. Furious that his influence has been destroyed, he stabs his master to death. The better self has conquered, but the baser self has its revenge.

Part of the effect of the play lies in the contrast between the disaster itself and the characters' unawareness that disaster has occurred. Spectators are aware of the disaster as well as the horror, but the bride is oblivious, happy and gay, and the bridesmaids laugh and make merry.

The use of the word "shadow" contributes to the poetic effect. A "shadow" becomes the term for the bridegroom's jealous fantasies when he imagines he sees a shadow in the moonlight gliding toward the door of the summerhouse; "shadow" is used to designate insubstantial individuals—adventurers and other disreputable types—while decency and honor are the criteria of substance, transforming shadows into flesh and blood.

The bride believes in the substance of her beloved shadow: "But tell me, don't you believe that a shadow has honor, decency —a conscience?" She reverts to the same concept of substance in her final lines when she has found Erik's dead body and finally grasps what has happened: "He has eyes, lips, breast, arms, hands. And you call him a shadow? He gave his life for honor. And to think you didn't believe it!"

Bergman was to return to the substance-giving function of honor. In the novel *Lady Gunhild at Hviskingeholm* he wrote of the revenge that can be taken by the shadows, by the inner, secret, forbidden life. He called the play "proverb" in the manuscript, thus intimating that he felt a kinship with Musset's bittersweet view of love and its interplay with guise and falsehood.

Bergman the dramatist was thus defeated for the time being: his own original approach had proved a fiasco. He had already written a comedy, called *Fusk* (*Cheating*), that was never performed. Now he reverted to comedy in a play rendered in a witty, intellectual style reminiscent of the writing of George Bernard Shaw. Entitled *An Experiment*, it is a conversational piece set in upper-class circles at the turn of the century. It deals with social prejudice and with an experiment performed on human material—not too far removed from the one Professor Higgins performed in Shaw's *Pygmalion*. In some of its basic ideas (wealth *versus* poverty), it recalls the philosophy of the weapons magnate in *Major Barbara*. The psychological symbolism, it is true, is Bergman's own, and the fundamental problem is also his, but the two do not easily blend into the witty, intellectual style he was intending. Shaw was rational and optimistic: Bergman was irrational and pessimistic, and the mixture was not a happy one. Notwithstanding, the play was a success when it was produced in 1919.

Still another playful piece—which Bergman himself liked—was *Friarna på Rockesnäs* (*The Suitors at Rockesnäs*), set in Bergslagen. This is a game in the moonlit garden and park of a manor house. The dialogue, partly in verse, is intended to unmask the false, flowery language in which love is wrapped for purely selfish motives. But the author decided it was not worth the trouble even to send the manuscript to a producer. *Lodolezzi sjunger* (*Lodolezzi Sings*, 1918) has more substance: it is a divertissement about a famous opera singer, who has married a stupid prince and given up her career. The play captures the excitement generated by her decision to return to her art and her admirers—for at least one glorious performance. *Lodolezzi Sings* has been produced on several occasions with considerable success, but it remains scarcely more than a skillfully devised lark. Still it has a bitter-serious core: the relationship of artists to their art, their inner motives for devoting themselves to this form of vanity, and their dependence on the audience and its taste.

The next play published is a significant landmark in Bergman's growth as a dramatist: it is closely related to his marionette plays and was probably written as early as 1916; with it he took another step in the direction of symbolism and became, in fact an expressionist. *Spelhuset* (*The Gambling House*) is a radical experiment in dramatic technique and a highly personal work of art.

What is new here is that Bergman, who had always expressed himself in highly symbolical terms, created a setting or an arena intended to represent the entire *span of life*.[2] Shortly thereafter Pär Lagerkvist (later a Nobel laureate) tried to achieve the same perspective on human life in a number of plays.[3] In Germany it became a common expressionistic approach, but Bergman appears to have pioneered it in Sweden.

The "Gambling House" is the arena in question: a place where the game is rigged, the manager is dishonest, innocence is debauched, and young people who enter in hopeful anticipation are robbed, only to return as aged beggars. (It is quite possible today to see it as a picture of capitalist society!) The step from *Mr. Sleeman Is Coming* is admittedly short in terms of content; but the former could be regarded as a psychologically realistic play whereas reality is consistently stylized in *The Gambling House*.[4] The characters are known as "The Manager," "The Friend," "The Bejewelled Old Lady," and "The Lady with the Roses." "Cocottes," "Gamblers," and "Assistants" are merely numbered.

Strindberg, to some extent, followed the same pattern in

the dream plays. The impulse to write in this symbolist fashion may have reached Bergman by way of Max Reinhardt's triumphal productions of Hofmannsthal's *Everyman* in Stockholm in 1915 and 1917. Bergman's brother-in-law, the stage director Per Lindberg, was extremely interested in Reinhardt and had worked with him in Stockholm for a time. Nevertheless, it is clear that the theme is closely related to the novel *Memoirs of a Dead Man*: the casino called Hotel de Montsousonge has several features in common with the gambling house.

The inner quality that implies a very close association between the two works is a kind of restrained optimism in the midst of the sombre, uncompromising vision. *The Gambling House* contains two flesh-and-blood characters,[5] the young lovers Karin and Gunnar. They represent innocence in the diabolical story, and they escape destruction. Thus, there is a very faint intimation of the possibility of deliverance by other means than death.

A few years passed before Hjalmar Bergman returned to playwriting. His next play, which he hid in a desk drawer, was as daring a scenic experiment as *The Gambling House*. Called *The Legend*, it was an examination of the myth of love, the concept in which Bergman believed as a young man and which he had tried to realize in his solitary life with his wife. But in the present context it is the form of the play that is interesting. The Legend herself appears on the stage as a symbolic female figure, invisible to the other actors. She dances and delivers monologues to the audience, comments on the plot and the character of the actors in roguishly lyrical terms. She is not only the legend of the manor house: she is fantasy itself, idealism liberated from the flesh.

Most of the members of the Ehrenstål family are down-to-earth, money-loving, practical people who believe in neither legends nor love. Sune, the squire of the manor, cherishes the legend attached to his home and to a spring in the grounds: that of a young woman whose love was so great that she gave her life in order to free her beloved to take another woman. The plot has two targets. One is the individuals who are excessively sober and calculating, those who have no use for legends; the other is Squire Sune, romantic to the point of self-delusion: he is forced to acknowledge his own idealization of love, his dream of submission, through the realization that his love contains elements of cruelty and lust for power. Love is not only idealistic surrender. The Legend suffers defeat in the play. Yet, events and discussions—romantic or manipulative—are wreathed in the Legend's poetic garlands. Realism is contrasted with the mythical in most effective fashion; the play is one that Ingmar Bergman has particularly enjoyed directing.

Another play which is also concerned with moral and intellectual issues is *Vävaren i Bagdad* (*The Weaver of Bagdad*), staged in an Arabian Nights setting. Here there are no miracles, no invisible characters; nevertheless, events are dominated by a fairy tale atmosphere. Caliph Harun el Rashid holds the power in his hands. A false caliph appears on the scene, is discovered and duly punished. The motif of the play is the contrast between blind power, arbitrarily exercised, and the demands of justice and compassion. The basic question: how does one recognize goodness and freedom?

The Caliph toys with the blind weaver's illusions of the beauty of the fabrics he is creating; he even considers whether the man should be penalized for his dreams; he is the ruler, and to him the concept of goodness is irrelevant (except as an occasional whim). The weaver's empty boasts represents human "life lies," people's fantasies of self-importance adopted to veil life's misery, which, unmasked, would kill them. All those who, in their blind ambition, their lust for life, have been punished or incapacitated by the Caliph still persist in believing in their imaginary greatness till the day of their death: the singer who cannot sing a note; the doctor who as a joke was promised all the Caliph's riches and is now mad with greed; the swordmaker now afflicted with the "shakes"; the blind weaver who believes he is the world's greatest artist in his endeavor—even though his fabrics are nothing but miserable rags.

Into this world of meaningless bondage bursts the young

Frank, René le Furieux, an adventurer without name or reputation, an unknown vagabond but a Westerner. In the last act, when the Caliph has dispensed his own brand of justice, punishing not only the arrogant rogue who played Caliph but also the dreamers—for their dreams—and the unhappy—for their misfortunes (which he himself had inflicted on them)—it is René who personifies the soul of the Western World, in contrast to the Orient. Will is free, he asserts (in the sense that it is free to be good). If it were on the side of evil, on the other hand, it would be a slave of lust and desire. One might say that the play is an interim answer to the question that Bergman posed earlier and to which he replied in a different way; it is related to the new sense of freedom he had won in 1919–1920.

The Portal (also written in 1920) gives additional answers to questions that had long been troubling him. It is a variation on the themes of departure and death. The portal is death's door, the door through which Henrik, a bitter and disappointed man, is to pass. On the other side of the portal he finds that everything has changed, his view of himself and his own guilt, of friends and foes alike. The play has key importance in the understanding of the author's personal philosophy: its contents will be discussed in the last chapter of this book. In terms of form, *The Portal* may be called the third of Bergman's expressionistic plays; yet it is ultimately a dream play: the intent is to look back upon life and consider its meaning, ponder its conditions, arrive at the total sum of wisdom.

The Gambling House, The Weaver of Bagdad, and *The Portal* were published in one volume in 1923. The critics were not only skeptical; they were downright negative. Again Bergman had been obscure, not to say unintelligible. Trusted friends urged him to write plays "in the same style as his novels." Theater managers gave him the same advice.[6] By their reference to the novels, his well-wishers probably meant that the plays needed a more realistic surface, with entertaining events, colorful characters, and sparkling witty lines. True: *God's Orchid* and *Herr von Hancken* fulfilled these criteria. They were fundamentally symbolic and relatively difficult to penetrate, but few critics or members of the audience seemed to notice.

These friends' recommendations presumably influenced Bergman's decision in the spring of 1923 to launch *Swedenhielms*, a play that in many ways responded to their wishes. It was realistic comedy, its dialogue was witty, its main character was "congenial." Quite simply, Bergman had written a rather conventional comedy, and some of the characters were typical to the point of being slick.[7]

Despite this, the play contains some magnificent scenes. It is a bravura piece with a bravura roll: the inventor Swedenhielm, impecunious, impractical, grandiloquent, but also ingenious and amusing. He is surrounded by spoiled children with great pretentions: a beautiful actress, a young officer, an engineer who is his father's assistant. All live beyond their means. The person who holds the widower's household together is Marta Boman, his sister-in-law and housekeeper. In the play, Swedenhielm is awarded the Nobel Prize, which should offer him an opportunity to clean up his financial mess. But suddenly, on the great day, Eriksson, a money-lender and old school friend, turns up. Systematically, he had been purchasing promissory notes signed with the name of Swedenhielm—including a few forgeries—which had been circulating among his colleagues. One purpose of his visit is to collect the money owing to him, but another of his purposes is more important: to discover how Swedenhielm would judge the crime of forgery. For Eriksson himself had once received, for a minor offense, a stiff sentence from Swedenhielm's father. The sentence had shaped his destiny. Swedenhielm, of course, offers a lofty harangue about his honor and puts on an act of being a famous, successful nobleman—until suddenly he realizes that someone in his family is guilty of forgery. In the end it turns out that the housekeeper committed the forgeries—to spare the great, extravagant man worries over petty money matters.

The moral of the play—"deliver us from vainglory"—is so well concealed among Swedenhielm's bravura arias that it is seldom perceived by audiences, even though the work has been performed thousands of times in Sweden and abroad. The play presents an airy discussion about what is base and what is noble in society. It deals with pride and humility in very ingenious fashion: perhaps this seldom-observed message has nevertheless contributed to the exceptional success of the play.

It was not surprising that Bergman continued along this new road, even though he was to write very few entirely new plays during his remaining years. He dramatized *God's Orchid,* first for the radio and later for the stage, and then *His Grace's Last Testament.* Both were effective and popular plays. Some of the finesse of the characterization, some of the symbolic overtones of the novels, were lost in the transition, but the main characters became classics, a part of the Swedish idiom for years to come.

The Rabble, Bergman's comedy on a Jewish theme, was written in 1928 under the lengthening shadow of Hitler and anti-Semitism. It was also a great success. The leading part, that of the imaginative businessman Joe Meng, was written for Gösta Ekman, who played it in the original production. The story tells of a family who had emigrated from Eastern Europe to Northern Germany. They pay an unexpected call on a rich relative, an antique dealer, who sends a message that he is out of town. Joe nevertheless inveigles his way into the house and, in his uncle's absence, takes over his business. A rich and stupid count makes a play for Joe's daughter, but is turned down in no uncertain terms. A porter thinks he has been undertipped. The two episodes cause trouble, and a minor pogrom breaks out. No great damage is done, family ties remain unbroken, the rich relative returns home—actually he has been observing events from rather close quarters—and a great reconciliation takes place. But ingenious Joe Meng is constantly cooking up new projects. According to Bergman himself, the play is intended as a study of Jewish fantasy. And the plot is indeed rich in fantasy, with the love story of two young people, the music of a young violinist, grandfather's words of wisdom and biblical quotations; all are woven into a plot that hovers on the borderline between fantasy and harsh realism.

In fact, a complete novel unfolds between the first and last act. This is also true of Bergman's other plays of the 1920s (after he had put aside his experiments with form). They are plots with a fairy tale element, intricately constructed plans of action featuring powerful scenes in which the characters bare themselves to the point of total surrender, leaving the audience halfway between tears and laughter. They no longer provide new directions for drama, but they are nevertheless inimitable in their inventiveness. The same is true of *Dollar*, Bergman's last play, which is marred by the fatigue he felt toward the end of his life; it suffers from a somewhat mechanical treatment of events and dialogue, a certain emptiness. But this play, too, reveals some of the features I have just mentioned: Bergman's scenic ingenuity, his ability to create tragicomedy. His characters are never run-of-the-mill. With bold fantasy, they illustrate the tragic implications of life, its painful complexity, but also humanity's comical, pathetic, or touching attempts to control destiny.

CHAPTER 13

Was Bergman a Social Critic?

IN the 1920s Victor Svanberg,[1] a well-known Swedish critic, wrote that Hjalmar Bergman was the voice of the decaying bourgeoisie. This characterization stemmed from the social and political discussion current at the time; and Svanberg tried consistently to prove that art and literature are relatively direct expressions of the society in which they are created.

This theory was presented in order to prove that Bergman's stories applied only to a "moribund class." The critic claimed that the strong determinism in Bergman's novels, a sort of melancholy fatalism, could be explained by a sense Bergman must have had of belonging to a decadent, formerly powerful group. His experience of the injustice and degeneration of the bourgeois capitalist world could be regarded as one explanation for the neurotic element in his works. Deliberately or unconsciously, his books amounted to accusations.

Victor Svanberg's analysis gave rise to considerable discussion. Wasn't Bergman an exceptionally impartial writer? Wasn't he primarily a psychologist? The opposition dismissed Svanberg's claims as doctrinaire Marxism.

Svanberg was neither doctrinaire nor Marxist: but he regarded himself as a socialist and was critical of bourgeois liberalism. With the passage of years, it has become clear that his theory about Bergman was partially true. The farther we come from the turn of the century and the prewar years—and much of Bergman's writing was done before 1914—the clearer it becomes that even though the social order this man's works reflect belongs to the past it remains significant to us for its aftereffects. We may emphasize the "rottenness" of this order

123

less than Svanberg did; we may speak less dramatically about "decay." But we cannot deny that the society described by Hjalmar Bergman has dropped below the horizon. It has been transformed. With his realistic approach, he records the transition between nineteenth century liberalism and what is considered today the Swedish welfare state. His sense for detail allowed him to capture characteristic qualities in rich measure; the period in which he lived—which put him within earshot when socialists sharply criticized prevailing conditions—gave him a critical perspective on what he observed.

But to call Bergman a deliberately political or socially tendentious writer is another matter altogether. Undoubtedly he viewed himself primarily as a psychologist and a symbolic portrayer of life and only secondarily as a chronicler of social conditions (particularly in novels such as *We Books, Krooks and Rooths*); but he would certainly have been the first to insist that the villainies and weaknesses he wrote about were typical of the human race as he knew it and that the symptoms of disease shown by bourgeois society would presumably be succeeded by other, morally comparable symptoms under a new and different system.

Seldom, if ever, either in letters or books, did he give any intimation of specific political sympathies. He was relatively interested in economics and enjoyed discussing business matters. He had a keen eye for social injustice, as evidenced in *We Books, Krooks and Rooths*, but he regarded them from an old-fashioned conservative and patriarchal point of view: they should be eliminated, but the initiative could just as well come from the old social classes as from the new.

There is much evidence to suggest that he distrusted politics. But certainly his perception of group and class conflicts was extremely acute—they were an integral part of human relations, about which it was his mission to write.

In one of his earliest works, *Solivro*, he depicted in fairy tale form the deep social conflict between a ruling people—the Aeretans—and an enslaved people—the Matretts. The description of the contempt that was felt for the Matretts (there was even an aura of disgust about their dwellings), contains a good deal of deliberate satire. A far-reaching battle for justice rages in *We Books, Krooks and Rooths*; in the *Loewen Stories* the ineffectual benevolence of the artist Loewen is manifest in his desire to eliminate class difference in the house in which he lives. There the rich live in apartments facing the street, the poor face the backyard, and a top-floor front location is top status. The house is a microcosm of society at large. *Comedies in Bergslagen* deals with a struggle between families, but it can also be said to concern exploitation, for the Siedels, one of the families, belong to the Bergslagen upper class while the Erse-Janse families consist of "ordinary" farmers and miners.

The later works do not always focus so sharply on groups or social classes. Bergman also tended to resolve conflicts into individual psychological or universal problems, or to show the complexity of the social struggle.

The comedy, *An Experiment,* illustrates the contrast between rich and poor in a very effective way that is very typical of Bergman—the technique is psychologically analytical and the writer is especially interested in suppressed truths. In the comedy Dr. Abel (a wealthy student of the problem of poverty) permits a fantast named Severin (an impoverished student of the problem of wealth) to take over his place for a time as master of the household: after all, he should have access to source material. Severin adjusts well to his new situation, Abel less so, but the "experiment" comes to an end when the two men's private weaknesses are exposed and their innermost secrets revealed. Severin's weaknesses are his many barefaced frauds, his lies about his life, and his resultant fear of having to produce his simple old mother. Abel's weaknesses are his illusions that riches and education are a guarantee against a person being truly base and that he himself, because of his intelligence, is incapable of unreasoning jealousy.

Thus, the idea is that all of us—poor as well as rich—have a weakness, a "poverty," to conceal, and that this secret failing is more important than all outward deficiencies in our lives. No trace of leftist bias here! But Mr. Severin, the poor bluff, has tuberculosis; rich Dr. Abel is an expert bully. The witty if somewhat artificial dialogue contains a number of apt remarks about the fatal importance of differences in material conditions, about the shabbiness and constriction in the lives of the poor.

Thus, the contrasts in Hjalmar Bergman's books sometimes have a social origin. The nobility is opposed to the bourgeois, the rich to the poor, the educated to the uneducated: these opposites counter one another most effectively in *God's Orchid* (master to servant, banker to farmer or businessman). The society he depicts has clearly marked boundaries and strongly defined interests. It is a world in which roles are firmly fixed, but in which unexpected reversals of roles may occur and in which the old, well-established families in a town suddenly find themselves deposed by strangers with crude manners, but with plenty of money earned in mysterious, suspect ways: prewar society, in other words.

It is difficult to determine the degree to which Bergman's psychological pessimism, his interest as a young man in apathetic, "crushed" protagonists, his unfailing eye for human predatory instincts, are rooted in specific experiences from his bourgeois environment. Certainly, he heard much talk of business, and the anecdotes sometimes concerned successful "killings" and the ruin of rich men. It is also true that many of the bourgeois tricks or financial methods he occasionally describes, in bitter, witty terms, were typical of the free wheeling capitalist society of that day. Arnfelt, the banker in *Memoirs of a Dead Man* and *The Kerrmans in Paradise*, is a genuine beast of prey, and his initials, A. O., were identical with those of a Swedish financier very prominent in that day. People used to say (we are told in *The Kerrmans in Paradise*) that his wide, pike-like jaws would often gobble "one fat citizen for breakfast, two foundry owners for dinner, and a bunch of well-peeled farmers for supper—then he picks his teeth with the Constitution."

Hjalmar Bergman's imaginary town was called Wadköping, his province Bergslagen—early counterparts of Faulkner's Jefferson and Yoknapatawpha County. Bergman was remarkably true to his environment. Of his twenty-two published novels—twenty-three including the one he wrote under a pseudonym—nineteen can be attributed to the Bergslagen world. Even if the story is not there, the characters are nonetheless members of well-known Wadköping families. In addition, we have *Death's Harlequin*, *Swedenhielms*, and *Dollar* plus a large number of short stories published in periodicals or collected in the volumes entitled *Love Through a Window* and *The Labyrinth*.

This fact in itself establishes his attachment to one particular social milieu during one particular period of time. The great majority of characters belongs to a small town version of Swedish bourgeoisie, either at the beginning of the twentieth or during the course of the nineteenth century. Some of the stories from the 1920s give the impression of belonging to the period. Foundry-owners, bank directors, and big businessmen dominate the scene in his books. Business deals and more or less ambitious financial projects are usually featured prominently, and the story is a merry-go-round of inheritances, purchases, estates, and companies. On the other hand, Hjalmar Bergman seldom wrote about artists—the most important exception is *Jac the Clown*. Only on rare occasions did he write about scholars: characters in *Swedenhielms* and *The Girl in the Dress Suit* are exceptions.

Aware of this fixation, he referred in letters to his "bourgeois milieu." He endowed the unpredictable and often difficult clown Jac Tracbac (his *alter ego* in a sense) with a certain bourgeois propriety in manners and dress, and he took pleasure in describing situations in which the clown closely resembled his merchant forebears. On one of his first appearances in the book, Tracbac is posing for a portrait in a historical costume. "He wore a high starched collar, an ample flowered stock, a black redingote, and narrow nankeen trousers. A thick watch-chain bearing a cluster of seals spanned his stomach. He looked like a member of the Royal Board of Commerce or some other pillar of society in the first half of the nineteenth century." But in fact the game is serious. Spiritually, the author himself had often worn similar garb. At the same time, we are given rather a good picture of Bergman's impressions of the outward appearance of Borck and Bourmaister, both characters important businessmen in some of the earlier books.

To appreciate the presence of bourgeois elements in his stories, we need only recall the role played at the time by convention, by Wadköping's officious gossip and inflexible pecking order. Some of the rules are broken by Bergman's characters—which causes an uproar—and these seem antediluvian today. The father-patriarch is the dominant figure in every family. Hjalmar Bergman describes counts and barons, with a dash of bourgeois satire, in about the same way as the respectable citizens of Örebro talked over the antics of the proud, noble families on their country estates. From an eighteenth or nineteenth century perspective, the Counts Arnfelt seem like rural despots. Their powerful descendants, the Wadköping bank president with the initials 'A. O." who lived in the nineteenth century, had, like Swedenhielm, taken up a completely bourgeois way of life. Thus, while the nobility is either characterized by means of middle-class satire or else rendered as a sort of superior bourgeosie, the upstart is scrutinized more keenly, with the special awareness of bad upbringing and unbecoming habits that is the heritage and privilege of the well bred. Markurell speaks in dialect, his jokes are coarse, he shuffles around in thick yellow socks, he washes seldom and gingerly, with due precaution. He is depicted realistically, it is true, and oddly enough he is finally transformed into a kind of saint. But the unbelievable or unexpected aspects of this transformation are credible when seen through the sharp eyes of a well brought up bourgeois.

Prosperous, comparatively well-educated middle-class business families, with relatively fixed "upper" and "lower" boundaries, thus constitute Hjalmar Bergman's human subjects. They make up the dominant group in Wadköping and Bergslagen.

Considering this, it is no coincidence that *God's Orchid* gives (among other things) a telling description of the frantic pursuit of the "white cap," symbol of the matriculation examination. This particular symbol may be a thing of the past, now that the form of the examination has been changed. The caps were sought after by parents who wanted to give their children a better start in life than they themselves may have had—but also to provide tangible proof of a solid financial background and a good social standing. It was around the turn of the century that men of Innkeeper Markurell's type began to give their sons secondary education instead of taking them into their own trade straight from grade school.[2]

As I have already indicated, the clash or "class struggle" between the two categories of bourgeoisie—the educated solid citizens with inherited fortunes, on the one hand, and the intruders, the self-made Markurells, on the other—is made beautifully clear in Bergman's books. He observed this social confrontation through the perspective of his personal experiences in Örebro. But in reality this conflict was only a part of the longer, larger struggle toward Swedish democracy (marked politically by the introduction of universal suffrage in 1918).

Unquestionably, the premise on which this process was founded was the liberal philosophy of economics, the system created by the bourgeoisie itself.

Even if Bergman's observations were not made from such lofty perspectives, they were no less acute. "It sometimes seems to me," he wrote in an essay about the region in which he spent his childhood, "that Örebro is like a besieged city, surrounded on all sides by powerful, stubborn countryfolk. The toll gates are penetrated by a steady stream of small groups of young men armed with axes and saws, hammers, chisels, and diverse weapons. They don't look particularly warlike, but the old bourgeois families nevertheless must move aside, hand over the power and authority to the newcomers, who scarcely have time to do a day's work, build their house, and settle down before new waves of intruders demand room and work and authority in this constantly besieged city."

In his essay "Örebro People I Know and Örebro People Who Are Well Known," Hjalmar Bergman noted that the city had "remarkably few families who had stayed at the same social level for several generations." At the same time, he gave the immigrants a pat on the back: "A sharp-tongued stranger once called this ancient, venerable Örebro a 'city of upstarts.' So be it, good brethren! There is a considerable measure of honor in the term and hope for the future also."

This could be regarded as sociological observation. But it may be appropriate here to recall a dozen lines from *God's Orchid* in which Bergman, through a few keenly observed details, describes the career Markurell, the upstart, slowly carves out for himself in Wadköping.

Mr. Markurell's social position in Wadköping underwent changes, but remained somewhat indeterminate. There was said to be a time when he was offered a cup of coffee in Judge de Lorche's kitchen. Later he drank it in the housekeeper's room, still later sitting at a corner of the dining room table. And the time came when, as a member of the board of the Wadköping Metal Works Inc., he dined at the same table in formal evening dress, wearing the insignia of the Vasa Order. His position changed, but he himself stayed the same. He still ate with his knife, he still scratched his fringe of red hair with grubby fingernails.

Bergman professed or let his characters profess a sexual ethic that was typical of his class and of the time in which he lived. Those who kicked over the traces were fully aware of what was right: revolts against convention were scarcely typical of that day. He himself was in many respects a rebel, and he wrote, with the most profound insight, of the inner struggle with forbidden lusts. But he always felt a strong loyalty to the rules, and his revolt was never entirely overt. Bergman hints that Jac the clown had roots in his forefathers' milieu: he emphasizes the clown's refusal to introduce the slightest off-color element into his acts. Bergman himself was not so strict. A critic once wrote of *Ljung, Medardus and I* (after having reviewed *Eros's Burial* the previous year) that beauty has many faces, that indecency is one of them, and that Bergman was a master of the indecent. This, of course, was a somewhat gross misinterpretation.

In his novels, Bergman was fond of erotic jest, of reference to sexual matters, and in *Ljung, Medardus and I* he tried to describe the awakening sexuality among young people and Wadköping's narrow-minded concept of morality. Much of the plot concerns a scandal caused by little Hannele's appearance in a classical play, at the Wadköping theater, dressed in an overly short shift. This indeed implied criticism, a revolt: indignation at the small town mentality that could start a smear campaign on such petty grounds. But in no sense does the revolt sweep away all the old ideas. The boys' attitude to the girl is chivalrous and devoted, and the feelings of the protagonist Love for Hannele are the epitome of romantic adoration.

As an artist, Bergman analyzed eroticism, emphasizing the sexual aspect. But his analysis was concerned primarily with the subconscious life of the spirit: instinct, yearning, the smoke of extinguished fires, but rarely the blazing flame itself. A possible exception would be *The Head of the Firm*, but this novel no doubt represents the most restrained demonstration of psychoanalytical theory ever written. The road toward a new form of decency, a frank approach reflecting a new code of morality, was not paved until later—in Sweden mostly by writers of a social class different from Bergman's.

It is true: as a writer Hjalmar Bergman was free from purely conventional ideas of honor. But he was capable of paying them homage, of formulating them in a voice vibrant with emotion. Also he saw through them. An interesting example appears in the definition of honor in *Swedenhielms*. The great inventor, the leading character, has certain principles of honor which are in no sense unconventional—one of them is that an engaged couple should be on an equal footing financially. This is a matter of pride, etc. But honor means honesty, first and foremost. Honor and happiness go hand in hand. The monologue about honor is one of the high points of the play, and it could scarcely have been written if Bergman had not sympathized with the noble sentiments it expresses. His destiny—*mutatis mutandis*—resembled that of another great writer of bourgeois origin: Thomas Mann. He, too, depicted his milieu; he, too, broke away in order to find freedom; he "rebelled." But when it came to taking a moral stand, it was obvious that his roots had never been completely severed.

Nonetheless we should keep in mind that the monologue about honor reveals a kind of hubris in Swedenhielm. As the play proceeds, it becomes clear that he has been able to remain immaculate only by hovering above the problems of everyday existence in absentminded ignorance. His uneducated sister-in-law/housekeeper is forced to forge promissory notes to keep the household afloat. Who is the real culprit? In principle, proud Swedenhielm is not much better than Eriksson, his old school friend who suffered dishonor as a youth and now wants to find out whether Swedenhielm is any more human, more broad-minded than his father, the judge. Eriksson, a convicted criminal, and Swedenhielm, crowned with laurels, are brothers under the skin: this is the moral intimated in the play. And thus the bourgeois facade is first illuminated and ultimately penetrated.

I mentioned Thomas Mann. Certain aspects of Hjalmar Bergman's work unquestionably remind us of the great portrait artist of the German bourgeoisie. As I have already shown, the influence of a practical, forceful, and demanding father on a son with a delicate nervous system is one of Bergman's favorite themes. It is an important motif in Mann's *Buddenbrooks* also. The subtitle of Mann's novel is *The Decay of a Family*; Hjalmar Bergman, in *Memoirs of a Dead Man*, describes the decay of a family through a sort of hereditary curse. For Thomas Mann, death, as in *Death in Venice*, was a motif with decadent appeal, a sinful temptation; for Bergman, too, the death motif was of utmost importance, with a flavor of decadence in *Memoirs of a Dead Man*, the chronicle of a family.

A recurring theme in Mann's work is the artist's congenital alienation from bourgeois existence; in Bergman the same theme is first intimated in *Ma at Sutre Inn* and then more pronounced in *Thy Rod and Thy Staff* and *Jac the Clown*.

But the longing of the artist and outsider for an everyday existence, for "life in its seductive banality" (Mann confessed to this in *Tonio Kröger*) is not foreign to Hjalmar Bergman. In his portrayal of the solid and pious Squire Längsäll—who returns from the fields after a hard day's work with his arms around his oxen's necks—he created not only an aesthetic contrast to the clown's artificial, rootless existence. He etched an unforgettable picture of his own longing and that of the clown for a solid, closed world.

To his readers, Hjalmar Bergman's "Bergslagen" is more of a spiritual concept than a geographical one.[3] It sometimes signifies an atmosphere, an eccentric quality often displayed by his characters. But this special trait may well be associated closely—and freely—to certain geographical and historical realities, to certain traditions of Bergman's childhood, to an extravagant style of life which used to be attributed to this rather wealthy part of Sweden. Here the term refers to the specific environment reflected in the majority of Bergman's novels and short stories, emphasizing sometimes the social and sometimes the local aspect.

The importance of the locality should thus not be disregarded. In terms of literature, Hjalmar Bergman discovered this region of Sweden. The mining communities described by Selma Lagerlöf lay farther to the west in the province of Värmland. The ancient mining world of Nora and Linde was resurrected in his books. The trade route leading to Stockholm from the mines in Västmanland, Närke, and Värmland *via* the port of Örebro on Lake Hjälmaren was of vital importance to Sweden's economy for centuries, and now a literary monument was finally erected to commemorate it. The city of Örebro itself, as the capital of Bergslagen and a center of a prosperous region with many large farms and estates, was immortalized in his writings.

At the same time, the old, traditional iron and leather market,

St. Henrik's Fair, was given poetic life. It made its début in
literature at the very moment when its economic importance
had begun to wane. Much solid historical knowledge and
accurate information about a powerful past are concealed in a
tumultuous, fantastic series of events.

As I intimated in the biographical chapter, any description
of the introduction of "Bergslagen" to Bergman's writing begins
with St. Henrik's Fair. Bergman never concealed the importance
of the two annual fairs (one in the fall and one in the winter)
to his vast repertoire of characters and settings. The life of the
marketplace was a general stimulus to his imagination. "The
Giant who wants to feel Mother Svea's pulse," he wrote, "should
place his hand over Örebro. A marketday. . . ." He devoted long
reminiscences to the town of his boyhood. He wrote, in reference
to the town's significance:

Örebro was a trading town. Grain dealers, tanners, leather merchants, dairymen handled a great part of the produce of the countryside. The livestock market was and probably still is [this was written
in 1930] a busy one. In my day, cattle and squires, farmer, butchers,
and merchants gathered in the fields south of the town. The mooing,
neighing, snorting, chattering, and bartering were highly attractive.
Gypsies and other horse dealers often turned up by families and clans
and were admired in all their romantic tawdriness.

These lines applied to the fall market on Michaelmas Day. But
the January market commemorating St. Henrik in the Middle
Ages was even closer to Bergman's heart. The former was of
primary interest to housewives while the latter was of a more
industrial character. Bergman, who called it the Mineowners'
Parliament of Sweden (or Central Sweden), describes it in
terms that reveal what an impression it must have made on
him as a ten-year-old boy.

For Örebro, St. Henrik's Fair was a kind of leftover from the
halcyon days of the Christmas season. The glow and festivity that
were put aside on St. Canute's Day [January 13] enjoyed a brief, brilliant aftermath in the last part of January.

This pleasurable annual occasion provided the young writer with an understanding of life and people, and the following passage suggests why:

> There were certainly few homes that were not touched in one way or another by the invasion of strangers from nearby. The wealthier families gave more or less brilliant parties for relatives and friends from the neighborhood, and the poor took in lodgers either for money or for the sake of friendship.

Hjalmar Bergman's family belonged to the wealthier category. But that was not all. His banker father had connections with everyone and conducted business throughout the province and even in the neighboring provinces. His house was crowded with guests on the days preceding and following January 19. And to his quiet, precocious son—with whom he often talked business as he would with adults—this show was a feast for the eyes, ears, and all the senses. As a result of this unusual relationship the father took the boy with him wherever he went and this had a special significance in connection with St. Henrik's Fair. In the 1890s the boy, as I have mentioned before, accompanied his father to *Sällskapet*, the clubroom in the city's leading hotel where the important men of the fair used to meet on one or more of the evenings they were in town, and where time was passed in talking, drinking, and playing cards. It must have been a strange sight: the noise, excited businessmen, drinking, and talking; a lone, silent, plump little fellow sitting wide-eyed in a corner. A boy with cameras for eyes. In his own words:

> The foundry and estate owners who visited the town for the St. Henrik's Fair belonged to the province and to neighboring provinces. I imagine that the glow emitted by the town's plutocrats, civil servants, and army officers on the other festive occasions, such as Oscar's Ball, paled somewhat when these supercilious gentlemen wrapped in magnificent furs passed through the city gates to the tune of opulent sleigh bells and the coachmen's arrogant cracking of their whips. I knew personally some of the men (inasmuch as a child can be said

to know an adult), and that is why I remember them better than
others.

After mentioning a couple of gentlemen by name and sketch-
ing them in a few words, he draws a more detailed portrait.
One of those he selects is Yngström at Valåsen.

This old man was accorded not inconsiderable respect by Turk as
well as Christian. He was a rather solitary .an, but I knew him
fairly well as a friend of my maternal g   dfather and a frequent
guest in my parents' home. He looked j·   like a Bergslagen troll,
short and broad, sharp-eyed, with extr   dinarily large ears and
mouth. In addition, an apparent bitternes. of character. He was regarded as one of Bergslagen's lords, the owner of great properties.
When the first electric power was to be brought in to Örebro from
the Bratt and Skråm waterfalls, he refused to allow the cable to
cross his land. This was the only possible route, and the old man's
obstinacy nearly put an end to the whole project. Fortunately, his
daughter hinted to my father that a personal call might change his
mind. My father set off, and I slipped along with him, too small to
be noticed but not too small to observe the exceptionally lovely
countryside and the terrifying but rather impressive old Bergslagian.
As it turned out, my father returned home the victor, which was
regarded as a miracle.

Similar expeditions and characters reminiscent of old man
Yngström are not unusual in the novels. Thus, the anecdote is
highly informative.

Only a few of the great many characters who somehow or
other became etched on the boy's memory, either *via Sällskapet*
or in connection with business trips in the region, were mineowners or foundry managers. Some were owners of big farms,
some were Örebro businessmen, but in any case men from the
plains. Nevertheless, the term Bergslagen constantly recurred
in their conversation, and their thoughts focused on mines and
foundries—to the young Hjalmar Bergman, the whole group
was made up of "Bergslagen fellows." This was the term applied

by the townspeople to these Knights of St. Henrik, regardless of their origin.

Naturally, in this untamed era, many of them were eccentrics. Perhaps not all of them could be called trolls, but old man Yngström was not the only one whose appearance was either peculiar or overwhelming. And the boy's psychological perception was certainly sensitive enough; not only was he amused at the grandiloquent phrases, the anecdotes and bursts of laughter, he also detected the calculation and stinginess concealed by jovial manners. Many of the anecdotes must have dealt with mines and business deals, success stories and sudden poverty. In most of them, the protagonist was probably only a name; many were almost legends. While some of these anecdotes from *Sällskapet* have been immortalized in the first two volumes of *Comedies in Bergslagen*, St. Henrik's Fair was given a monument more durable than bronze in the novel entitled *St. Canute's Fair*, the last of the *Comedies*.

But "Bergslagen" was not built in a day. It was certainly not Hjalmar Bergman's plan from the beginning to choose a permanent geographical setting for his stories or to confine himself to a limited number of families. Nor did the concept of Wadköping exist at the outset. Things happened as they usually do: one thing led to another.

The embryo was simply Örebro, his own hometown, and from it grew the town that gave birth to "Bergslagen" and that engaged his complete attention for years to come.

In *Blue Flowers*, one of his earliest works, he used a few Örebro details for background. This may have been a coincidence. The next step was taken in *His Grace's Last Testament* in 1910. But this book was envisaged primarily as a gallery of portraits. Since the main character was drawn from the author's memory of a particular model, many background details were inevitably a part of the portrait. Actually, this book contains a good deal of the world of "Bergslagen." At least two of the estate names, Klockeberga and Björkenäs, as well as family names like Siedel,

Hyltenius, and Lilja, were to recur in subsequent works. But there is practically no mention of foundries or mines.

The "town chronicle" next tackled by Bergman, *We Books, Krooks and Rooths,* was clearly intended to depict life and people in the anonymous neighboring town sometimes mentioned by His Grace. Bergman found details in old books of reminiscences and oral chronicles. But there was still no thought of "Bergslagen"; the town itself was the center of attraction. Not even the markets were yet of any importance.

The town played the main role in still another book with no particular reference to foundry owners or "Bergslagen" conditions; namely, *Loewen Stories.* It was not until his next work, a collection of short stories, that Bergman moved into a setting of foundries and mines although he retained the names of families and places he had made up earlier for the story of His Grace: Klockeberga and Björkenäs, for instance. It was as if he were searching for the history of these imaginary estates, which had aroused his curiosity, and he began with a legendary sixteenth century bailiff.

The first two volumes of *Comedies in Bergslagen* contained seven stories—it was here that "Bergslagen" first saw the light of day. What he does in the third volume, which deals with the market, is merely to assemble his entire precious collection of "Bergslag" characters in the "town," the town of the Books, Krooks, and Rooths, just as the real Bergslagians used to meet now and again in Örebro. Where and how would their meetings be arranged? At the market, of course.

Memoirs of a Dead Man, which features certain new individuals and families, is also set in the town. *But it is not exactly the same town.* So far there has been no mention of a bishop, but we now find ourselves in a diocesan capital with both a bishop and a cathedral, and with a high hill in the center of town. Örebro had neither a bishop nor a hill with a view, but Västerås, the town where Bergman took his matriculation examination, had both. The town is no longer anonymous; it has an initial, "W." That was in 1918.

Then, in 1919, Wadköping was born in the novel about Markurell. The town of "W." is now given firmer contours. It is made livelier and more amusing in one sense and more boring in another. Hjalmar Bergman now begins his deliberate satire of small-town life. For the first time, he describes satirically the negative aspects and the psychological pressures of life in a small town. This was due in part to his need for a more specific environment, a "hothouse" in which a plant as rare as Markurell could grow to its full stature and ugliness.

From then on, practically all his stories are set in an urban milieu, and "Bergslagen" becomes almost synonomous with Wadköping. For example, *Herr von Hancken,* the novel of 1920, is a historical excursion to the neighborhood of Wadköping. It is a period fantasy about Adolfsberg, a spa outside Örebro that was fashionable once upon a time. Toward the end of the 1920s, Bergman began increasingly to use modern surroundings and to set his novels and plays in Stockholm, Paris, or—as in the comedy *Dollar*—in a mountain resort. But he consistently maintained the tie to Wadköping in the form of family names and relationships. One can see that the characters' connections with their origins were rather similar to his own. For after his mother's death at the end of the 1920s, very few ties joined the restless, tortured storyteller in his hotel room to the idyll hedged in by rules and old-fashioned customs that was the Örebro of his father and mother, the Närke of his childhood.

Bergman himself probably did not regard 'Bergslagen" as a province, Wadköping as a small town. "Bergslagen" was the microcosm in which he had set all the tragedies and comedies of human life.

"Big cities may exist," this widely traveled man wrote, "but I have never seen one."

CHAPTER 14

Clown of Terror

"WHAT is a poet?" Søren Kierkegaard asks in one of the most familiar rhetorical questions in literature. He replies that a poet is a human being whose lips are shaped in such a way that when he or she gives tongue to sorrow and lamentation, it sounds like beautiful music. One might also ask the question: What is a clown? And the answer might be that a clown is a being whose body and lips are shaped in such a way that when innermost experiences—including tragedy, sorrow, and desperation—are expressed, they will resemble high-spirited jest, hilarious capers.

Hans Larsson, the philosopher and one of those who really understood Hjalmar Bergman, rightly observed that "clowning" was not something that Bergman could "drop" in order to be "like other people."[1] On the contrary, the high point of his clowning is often reached in the works in which one senses most strongly the "beat of the heart."

The portrayal of Jac Tracbac, which is found in two novels and one short story, reveals that Bergman was fully aware of the degree to which gravity and farce were interwoven in the fabric of his nature. When young Nathan Borck experiences the great shock of his life, the one that turns him into a clown, he is possessed by a terrible fear, mixed with sorrow. A friend is fatally injured during a performance. But Nathan's reaction to the accident is completely ludicrous: he bounces like a rubber ball, he turns cartwheels, he yells, all to the ecstatic applause of the audience. And this is the key to the comic sketches that will make his fame.

Nathan Borck expresses himself solely through ingenious,

140

bizarre tricks. Instead of using words, he puts on a small symbolic act. That is how his fantasy works. What motivates him to do the trick is an emotion that calls for release, but it is intertwined in an arabesque of fantasy and diversion. This framework implies a self-ironical distance from his own person, a critical objectivity that never flags. He has his own opinion, but he is always half prepared to adopt his adversary's view. The clown's instinct is not only to express himself in tableaux and sketches but also to be objective and generous, to see both sides of the picture. His irony sometimes seems discordant, sometimes gently humorous, sometimes interesting and bizarre.

I have already mentioned the episode that occurred when the clown received the fateful and insulting letter from Lillemor Längsäll, the love of his youth, back in Sweden, in "Bergslagen." The description of his reaction is a fine psychological study. To the casual onlooker, he seems distrait; he mutters to himself in a forced sort of way. But to Bergman and the reader, it is clear that he is the victim of an overwhelming emotion. His gestures are a means of self-defense.

Rush, who was watching him closely, said in an indifferent tone of voice: "You have a stain on your forehead, Jac." "A stain on my forehead," Jac repeated absently, taking a mirror from his pocket and inspecting himself. There was indeed a stain, but it took him several seconds to realize what it was. It was only two small spots of ink which had appeared when he pressed the letter to his perspiring brow. His anguish had been blended with Lillemor's. Suddenly he began to behave in a way that Rush did not and could not be expected to understand. He approached Rush, made a comical face, and whispered: "Watch out, little Abel, watch out for big brother. Can't you see what's on my forehead? It's the famous mark of Cain."

It is later explained that to Jac this was a macabre, but nonetheless reasonable association. But the episode was soon to be used as proof of Tracbac's mental aberration. The author adds: "Man knows very little about his neighbor and is well-advised to judge him as seldom and as humbly as possible."

At the beginning of the clown's grand tour, he surprises his audience by reciting his "clown's catechism," but it does not occur to him to deliver it except as another sidesplitting routine. He is in costume, he shakes his rattle, he cavorts, he jokes.

When he decides to tell his colleagues, in private, the truth about his life and situation, he sabotages a plan for a serious discussion and instead puts on an act for the board members. Longfellow, the Negro, and Axelsson, the handyman, bring in a picture measuring about three by six feet and covered by a cloth.

The picture was a charcoal drawing of a delicatessen or butcher shop with marble walls, marble counter, a marble floor covered with sawdust. A skeleton was suspended by the neck from a hook. From its jaws hung two banderoles like those engraved with the family motto on a tombstone. On one, the following words were inscribed:
"I am Tracbac"
On the other: "I was born a man—I lived a clown—I sold my heart—I died a pauper."
The men stand around, embarrassed, hesitant and silent. At a sign from the clown, one of them goes up to the picture. He quickly pasted over the picture, over the window, a sign on which he had just printed the words:
"Stock sold out—gone out of business. Jac Tracbac Syndicate, Ltd."

This confession of desperation and emptiness could have been expressed in many ways: lyrically, sentimentally, ceremoniously, or sadly. Like Hjalmar Bergman, however, Jac preferred caricature, allegory, a sketch: it was his nature. The audience might have been moved even more profoundly that way. In any case, its effect is highly complex. Shortly thereafter it is discovered that tough Abel Rush, impresario and friend, has collapsed in a fit of sobbing in one of the many small rooms in the clown's bungalow.

Many tragic events and experiences in Hjalmar Bergman's books are staged as if they were comical. Markurell begins to suspect the awful truth about his son and behaves like a sick man: in reality he looks like a clown.

Suddenly he turned around; he looked disgusting. His mouth sagged as if from a stroke, spittle oozed from the corners of his mouth, his eyes were red and swollen, and fat tears rolled down his cheeks, leaving grubby streaks.

A few minutes later, he seats himself on the safe he had just hurled into the mess of wrecked furniture, a miserable heap of rubble. He is truly Job, but he looks like a clown. It is the grotesque element that emphasizes the tragedy and makes it believable: human beings are rendered utterly defenseless by real suffering—and Markurell, the "troll," is a human being.

No man can behave with such dignity as the destitute and incompetent Herr von Hancken when he moves among the social luminaries at Iglinge Spa as if he were the noble proprietor of a great estate. But he is a knight of the order of the ludicrous, a skinny, strutting fellow with a big waxed moustache and a gloomy expression. He falls in love with a countess who turns out to be an impostor—inevitably the decrepit old fool (who has been boasting about his conquest like a rooster on a dunghill) catches a young rival in his lady's bedroom. But this man of empty pretentions is denuded to the point that he is no longer ridiculous.

I have already mentioned the artist Loewen's resemblance not only to Don Quixote but also to Chaplin: the helpless little man who tries to play a part, who genuinely wants to set things right but who actually has no conception of what he is getting into. Hjalmar Bergman became interested in motion pictures at an early point, and he tried to see all Chaplin's films as far back as the first decade of the century.

The relationship between comedy and tragedy, between the clown's innermost intentions, sometimes finds even more outrageous expression. Hjalmar Bergman's view of himself fluctuated between clown and visionary, between fantast and prophet. On one or two occasions in his youth, he used this tension to create stories of almost unbearable effect.

One of them is called *Arlecchinos dröm* (*Arlecchino's Dream*).

It is a shocking story about an Italian juggler who believes he
has been given a mission by Saint Francis. It begins on a
beautiful and gentle note with poor Arlecchino, who lives in a
cave, telling Colombina, his woman friend, about a strange
dream he has had; and this domestic and practical creature—
if one can be domestic in a cave—obviously believes in the lucky
significance of such nocturnal signs. But events soon progress
to devastating, total disaster.

The dream was indeed remarkable. Arlecchino dreamed that
he was the "cruel wolf from Agobio." This famous wolf is mentioned in *Fioretti*, the well-known anthology of legends about
Saint Francis (Chapter XXI). His savage jaws and his stomach's
lust have led him to commit wicked deeds—though in the dream
the wolf says that his misdemeanors have been misunderstood
and exaggerated—and now he has been gently and firmly ad-
monished by Saint Francis. In the guise of the wolf, Arlecchino
pleads: "Your Holiness, allow me to share in God's good will."
Good will is the objective and the dream.

It is obviously significant that the juggler believes himself
to be a wolf. This was the very first time that Hjalmar Bergman
used a buffoon as a symbolic figure—the device recalls Anatole
France in *Le Jongleur de Nôtre Dame*, and the relationship between juggler and artist is quite clear. Yet, why should an artist
say of himself, "I was a starving, rapacious wolf"? This is
clearly related to the author's frequent struggles with his own
aggressiveness, his quick temper. But still the wolf in the dream
does amusing tricks for children, doesn't frighten them. Terrified,
Colombina asks Arlecchino if he had injured the innocent little
ones in his dream. He shakes his head:

"Did I harm them? I didn't touch them, I'm sure of that. The more
I suffered from hunger, the more comical my leaps and bounds became. . . . But innocence, Colombina, no; there wasn't a hundredth of
a sequin's worth of innocence among all those people."

As we see, artistry and savagery (aggressiveness) are combined in the wolf—mention is made in passing of the lack of

innocence in the world. What is strange and characteristic is that the wolf performs tricks instead of obeying his savage instinct and his simple need to devour the audience. "I could have reached them in one leap. I could have filled my jaws and my belly. But I didn't touch them." Art—an outlet for savagery!

Despite his unnaturally peaceful behavior—for surely the evangelical dream of peace is totally unnatural in connection with a wolf—Arlecchino's dream wolf is severely reprimanded by the saint: "Thou hast behaved like a bandit and a murderer, and this whole country is thine enemy." The artist-wolf has met opposition and earned a bad reputation. The wolf implores the people to testify in his defense, but no one steps forward. "He has fooled us with his tricks; with evil design he has lured us into the woods. The wolf! The wolf!"

The saint then instructs him to sleep during the day; when night comes, he is to make use of his skills only to give people pleasure. "Need and greed, demands and broken promises they will forget; of all the things they have begged and asked for in vain, joy is all they will come to know."

These words recall Hjalmar Bergman's often expressed reverence for pure joy; they confirm that it is the artist who can dispense joy:

"The talent is great; use it for the glory of God; give these people such joy that they will follow thee through the darkness of the night and the perils of the forest, follow thee blindly to the top of the mountain. There wilt thou see the sun!"

A remarkable dream, indeed, and poor Arlecchino takes it in all seriousness. He gives a fantastic performance—as a preacher. He begins by mildly shocking his audience to capture their attention. Then he relates a simple truth about life for a few minutes, tells his listeners about their miseries and crimes, and finally delivers the message of salvation through joy. But the listeners, the very people who have been singled out and unmasked, are obviously furious. They mock and taunt the preacher, follow him to the top of mountain out of mixed motives, including anger, vengefulness, and rapacity. Together, they consume Colombina's meager stock of food, exploit the juggler's newly acquired serenity and gentleness by begging money from him. To cap it all, Rialdo, stealer of women, runs away with Colombina. The monk, Matteo, begins to castigate Arlecchino for blasphemy and finally forces him, in his total defeat, to acknowledge that Satan is his God.

Now the juggler rose from his bed of torture. He stretched his hands into the darkness and uttered in a loud voice:
"I profess myself a follower of Satan."
And when he had spoken these words, blood gushed from his mouth and his nostrils. And he fell to the ground and gave up the ghost.

At the beginning of the story, Arlecchino is a sort of Adam who lives with his Eve in a mountain cave and accepts an apple from the woman's hand. At the end, judging from the biblical phraseology, his suffering is comparable with that of the Redeemer.

And so all is chaos, misunderstanding, disaster. The juggler's dream, without the slightest connection to reality, led to his humiliation and death. But it *was* a dream of beatitude—of joy; he embraced it with all his soul, and he died for it as a martyr or a Christ.

Another frightening and sombre story, *Den falske Cristoforo* (*The False Christopher*), has a related theme. The principal character is not a juggler, but a runaway priest who is a murderer—thus a "wolf" once again. The dream of purity, of Christ, is here too. It is not deranged, as in Arlecchino; it is the *idée fixe* of a lunatic. So violent is the contrast between reality and dream. So violent is the struggle between the dream of goodness and the reality of the dreamer. To illustrate the warring elements, Hjalmar Bergman is compelled to create a grotesquery. And the grotesquery is deeply moving, at times even sublime.

After killing a fellow-student—an act of vengeance—the priest dons the dead Cristoforo's coat. He believes that he is now a "Cristoforo," a bearer of Christ, whose task it is to carry the Child Jesus across the river.

He takes lodgings in a small town in a hostel dedicated to Saint Catherine. Some of the lady guests become interested in the strange man. He learns from them that there is a miracle-working statue of the Infant Savior in the town. He immediately interprets this as a sign from heaven: he is to lead a sacred procession, bearing the Child Jesus in his arms.

The procession sets off, led by the priest followed by three ladies from the hostel and ten harlots from a local brothel. Not until he is inside the church, near the altar, after a series of wild capers, is the criminal lunatic finally apprehended by the gendarmes.

The point of the story is obviously to find a ray of good will and beauty in the midst of the absurd. Bergman finds beautiful words to describe Cristoforo's devotion:

He approached the altar, genuflected, rose to his feet, and opened the glass door. After three more genuflections, he stood on tiptoe and, with a smile on his lips, removed the Child from His niche.

He held Him aloft in both hands, like the Host or a chalice filled with the blood of the Redeemer.

He turned to face the congregation and said: "Dear ones, look now! And ye shall be my witnesses!

"I am carrying the Child Jesus, as God commanded me. I am carrying my great lord and master, Jesus Christ. I am carrying the beloved little Child of my heart high above my head, where He cannot be defiled by the dirty water in which my body shall drown."

Hjalmar Bergman's view of life was thus far from bright. He saw himself almost with horror, and he often regarded life and its inexorable mechanisms with dismay. At the same time, even as a young man and still more in his middle years, he preached the doctrine of good will as a paradox, and he had a genuine sense for joy, which he always regarded as a miracle.

He combined terror and gaiety in a strange alliance in Jac, the "Clown of Terror." But was it so "strange"? Is terror not a skillfully exploited factor in all kinds of entertainment? Is it not a reliable device in many comic films, with the comedian climbing walls and hanging by ropes high over the street? Terror and laughter go together. As a psychologist, Hjalmar Bergman knew very well what he was talking about, even though the reader may find his theories and examples exaggerated.

In *Thy Rod and Thy Staff*, the clown returns home to his old grandmother in Wadköping and tells her about his profession. He was "discovered" as a clown the time he was almost annihilated by terror. He looked like an idiot on that occasion, and he was inundated by success from that day on. His grandmother is skeptical: she doesn't like what she hears.

"What in the name of heaven do they laugh at? Is it amusing to watch an idiot?"

"Yes, of course that's amusing, isn't it?" he replied and looked surprised.

The clown understands the secret mechanisms better than his grandmother.

We may also recall part of the dialogue in *Death's Harlequin,* a play particularly relevant in this connection as it shows the way people become feverishly active, pleasure-seeking, even facetious in the presence of death and fear. Dr. Brising describes in suggestive terms a puppet show he once saw: "Harlequin's Bells." The point of the plot, he claims, was that all the mourners at a deathbed began to dance whenever Harlequin rang his bell.

"His bell had the marvelous power to make all who heard it dance. There was utter confusion around the deathbed, friend and foe joined hands and danced away from the dying man. [The doctor comments that he recognized this show from his own marionette theater.]

"I've seen it so often—so very often. I—the death-doctor. Lips parting to pronounce a blessing twist into a sneer. Gentle eyes glitter at a

malicious remark or an obscene jest. I've thought to myself: now
Harlequin is ringing his bells and bewitching us. Hands which should
be supporting a dying person—I've seen them used for furtive pur-
poses. . . ."
Tyra (distressed): "Why? Why . . . "
"Because Harlequin is funny and death is awful."

It is thus the desire to flee, to escape from fear that is the
cause of people's excessive pirouetting, their daring flights of
fancy.

As I have pointed out before, Hjalmar Bergman was deeply
concerned with aesthetics. As a young man, he gave a series
of lectures on the subject, in which he dealt at length on the role
played by anxiety, sorrow, and anger in the aesthetic experience.
"Anxiety," he said, "is also an essential factor in the emotion
that is perhaps best suited to have a profound effect on our
spiritual life: namely, tension."

At the same time, his use of the word "joy" on this occasion
was no less personal. He believed, for example, that admiration
was a kind of joy. Admiration is part of the enjoyment of art,
and enjoyment of art as such is also a joy. Intuition, too, is
joy—and the religious experience! The monk who, in the space
of a silent second, sees his entire faith and his religious awareness illuminated by a great and powerful idea is possessed by
"intense joy at the sublime that could be encompassed by his
soul." Bergman also pays tribute to the special position of joy
among human emotions: it does not fatigue, it only gives rise
to pleasure.

A few times in his life, Hjalmar Bergman expressed in this
way what might be called a mystique of joy. He found joy
completely inexplicable, even factually unjustified, but nonetheless a fact, a basic fact of life.

"I believe that life is meaningless, but not necessarily a bad
business," he wrote to a friend in 1906.

Furthermore, I believe that it provides all too many great possibilities
of achieving the priceless treasure known as joy. And by joy I mean

every physical and mental feat that is followed by a pleasureable sensation. A feeling of pleasure in the broadest sense, leaving room for much of what we normally call pain. Well, for me the meaningless squandering of energy is the "meaning" of life, and the joy of squandering is its goal.

Six years later he returned to the same theme in a letter to Klara Johanson, the critic—this as a reply to a comment she had made that he found objectionable:

One more thing: laughter and tears are physical processes, and there is no point arguing with you on this score. But it is another story if you deny joy. Joy is transcendental. An unknown element that can be the subject of many thoughts and many pens.

He expressed the same view in a speech to the students of Uppsala University in 1928, two and a half years before his death. And in an essay in 1930, the last, shattered year of his life, he wrote:

"Cherish joy, you who possess it! Respect joy, you who lack it. The very fact that joy exists should be a source of joy."

Terror and joy; tragedy and comedy. Despite the darkness that hovers over many of the Bergslagen stories, despite the "cat-and-mouse" world his characters usually inhabit, there is balance in Hjalmar Bergman's art though not a facile balance nor always a particularly pleasant one. Some people may feel the lack of an element of detente in his books, perhaps justifiably. But the question is whether they have read his work correctly, if they have read it all. Tragedy and horror lurk about in his writing more often than in the works of many others. He does not allow us to be depressed without adding a dash of comedy or irony; he does not allow us to laugh without showing us the obverse side of joy. This often results in the comedy being "clouded" and the tragedy "polluted," according to older aesthetic standards. But this posture, this double acuity of vision, is the foundation of his art. In his view, tragedy and comedy are next-door neighbors. They complement each other like the two sides of a coin. He needs them both if the whole picture is not to be a falsification in his eyes.

One of the more inoffensive but typical examples is Adolph von Hancken, the fat and imbecilic boy known as Adolphen, in *Herr von Hancken.* This lad is a not-too-distant relative of some characters in the works of Dickens. Adolphen's strange indolence, his incredible appetite and his regrettable indiscretion are equally remarkable and comically effective. Like Dickens, Bergman not only makes us laugh: he makes us think. In Adolphen's case, comments and hints cause the reader to ponder on the reasons for the boy's peculiarity. He is an imbecile. So be it. We recall in Bergman—as in Dickens—that imbecile children are regarded as pitiable, a disaster, a sorrow for their parents. To be fat and a figure of fun may be comical, but it is a tragedy for the victim. Compassion and understanding prevent a smile from becoming a guffaw.

It may be helpful to remember that Bergman himself was in fat Adolphen's situation as a child. True, he was far from an imbecile, but he was ridiculed for his fatness. Another boy in his class was in the same boat, but he appears also to have had some of Adolphen's imbecility. Hjalmar himself used to tell about the boy's more or less ridiculous and stupid behavior in school. But we can be sure that he drew parallels between what appeared to be merely amusing in his fat schoolmate's behavior and what he found to be purely tragic in his own case. For it was one and the same thing! The ridiculous is often some slight defect, perhaps even a deformity, "nothing to laugh at." A peculiarity of Hjalmar Bergman's gift was that his acute sense of comedy was matched by an equally acute sense of tragedy. He saw reality with two faces, and he was incapable of disregarding either one. This characteristic became most striking in his clown, Jac Tracbac.

My comments about clowns and clowning are equally applicable to the "fantastic" in Bergman's art. The two concepts are in a sense interchangeable. Much of the clowning has its origin in an overly rich and agile imagination. Certain critics have used the term "hysterical fantasy," "hyper-excitation"— true on occasion, but only rarely. At the same time, fantasy is the clown's most valuable asset and the source of his art.

Sometimes the author's message seems simply to be that humans should be judged with discretion. What appears strange may contain a surprisingly simple kernel of the commonplace. He is contending with the problem of reality and appearance.

"Sardanapal" is the title of a story in *Love through a Window*. It is so full of clowning and fantasy that it may not satisfy the casual reader. Sardanapal is the sobriquet or nickname or even *nom de guerre* of a man of "Bergslagen" origin. The story deals with the voyage he and his wife took to visit relatives, and the trip is depicted in every detail as if it were the voyage of an oriental potentate with his harem. No clue is given to the protagonist's real identity.

This is the beginning of the story. When the innocent reader has been thoroughly worked over by various naturalistic oriental odors, the scene suddenly changes completely. The loyal and unsuspecting newcomer to Bergman will certainly need to read the story more than once.

"The destination was Skullebo, a small farm belonging to Rogershus. The tenant's mother, Mrs. Hedström, was Sardanapal's mother-in-law. He himself had once borne the humble name of August Jonsson." The name could not be more typical of the Swedish peasantry.

The game proves bizarre and confusing to the reader. It turns out that the Hedström family suspects the rich flautist and horse dealer—in most respects a fantastic man—of mistreating their daughter Lotta. The atmosphere of the family gathering becomes bleak, and the Hedströms try to dig out the truth. The climax of the story, an episode as full of excitement as of morbid psychology and sadism, is simply a make-believe circus act put on by Sardanapal and Lotta with the four favorite horses featured in the cast. Fat, apathetic Lotta, dressed in tights, plays stooge to her animal-tamer husband. She is apparently in mortal danger and, while her family looks on in terror, she allows herself to act the docile slave of his vagabond, circus instincts. But the major surprise is still in store. It comes after the performance when Lotta sees Sardanapal making eyes at Cousin Little-Lotta. The apparently terrorized wife immediately attacks her husband physically; she berates him and beats him until he is humbled, resigned, black-and-blue. When questioned, Lotta replies that this is the first time: "Never before has there been any cause."

What is the essence of this remarkable Bergslagen story? First, the general discovery that the relations between Sardanapal and his wife were not what they seemed on the surface. Next, the more special revelation that the apparently subjugated wife is actually the stronger of the two. Their strange behavior concealed a rather common—and yet not *entirely* common—love between a man and a woman, including jealousy and all the rest.

What appeared to be an extreme form of male tyranny was simply voluntary submission on Lotta's part due to blind devotion. The only thing she cared about was her husband's fidelity; nothing else mattered. And while cruel Sardanapal risked her life in the circus act, he did so in the knowledge that he was skillful enough to avert danger. Properly treated, he too is as meek as a lamb. It is true that the picture contains an element of horror, cruelty, and "sadism," but it is not what the onlookers believed. And the marriage, this marriage that appeared to be on the verge of catastrophe, turns out to be exceptionally solid; the innermost nature of the bond may remain a secret, but it is strong.

No wonder that the surface level of the story is confusing, considering the proposition: you speculate, good people, you speculate about your fellow creatures, but you never know them, and reality eludes your speculations. No wonder that clowning, disguises, surprises succeed one another when Bergman approaches his personal problems. There is no question

that he comes close to the story of his own marriage in this
rather bizarre narrative. It too appeared strange—and yet for
years it was undoubtedly the story of two individuals' extraordinary dependence on one another. The more disguise, am-
biguity, and camouflage, the closer we come to the heart of
the matter: here we have the key to much of the "fantastic" in
Bergman's production.

Only rarely is Bergman's humor entirely free from bitter
undertones. When this does happen, young people are usually
involved. Two examples are the engagement episode in *Jonas
och Helen* (*Jonas and Helen*), written in his middle age, and
the story of Blenda and Jacob in *His Grace's Last Testament*
from his youth. His young people possess fantasy, always a
charming quality in his eyes, and innocence and freshness. He
is especially amused by their attempts to appear depraved,
experienced, or diabolical. It is for this reason that *Jonas and
Helen* is subtitled "A Study of Youth and Fantasy." Tenderness
and indulgence give a glow to the story, to the coltish youngsters
and their antics. Their dreams and their inept attempts to cope
with reality, their emerging personalities are handled with
tolerance and understanding.

Humor is a redeeming force in the principal characters, the
dominant figures. They are unmasked, but they are also forgiven.
The best example is perhaps Grandma in her incredibly funny
conversations with Our Lord, but the miserable Herr von
Hancken also undergoes a paradoxical rehabilitation in the end.
And Markurell is ultimately elevated to a kind of sainthood.

Bergman has a special gift for bringing out the selfless devotion that many of his characters often reveal as though
involuntarily through occasional losses of self-control. The
poignant trait in that old egoist His Grace (the Baron) is not
only his devotion to his madcap daughter, but also his undying
love for her mother, the perhaps slightly wanton Mimmi, whom
his family had prevented him from marrying. It is in her that
his plans for his will are rooted. In all its despotism, Grandma's
love for her little grandson Nathan is closely related to the

Baron's emotions—although eleven years separated the two works.

Ljung, Medardus and I is a good example of Bergman's sunnier side. In this novel about his youth he allows himself to joke about young love and youthful idealism even though he certainly takes them seriously. He knows how it feels. Personal experience colors the description of the relationship between Love (Louis), the first-person narrator, and his comrades, on the one hand, and the little actress Hannele, on the other. As always, the most delicate and ephemeral nuances are conveyed in the proximity of death.

Little Hannele, whose childhood and youth had been "pure hell," tries to convince the young know-it-all college boys of the existence of God and the immortality of the soul. She does this by staging a spiritualist séance. Let those doubters see for themselves! As she senses the approach of death, her faith is the most profound, simple reality. But, due to her naïvité, the manifestation is a farce, and she is fully aware of the fraud— this paradox is Hjalmar Bergman at his best.

When Hannele falls ill and is plunged into a state of deep spiritual distress at the thought of her wanton way of life and debauched adventures at Rogershus, she persuades tough Medardus himself to summon the minister from Ekersta. He comes to visit the unfortunate child, but first orders Baron Bernhusen —the girl's seducer—to stand bareheaded in the middle of the courtyard, as a kind of penance, while he himself communes with Hannele. The Baron obeys! The entire episode breathes vehement sympathy for Hannele, interspersed by unexpected impulses, and the minister's behavior is the epitome of simple gravity. In the midst of it all, Roger Bernhusen de Sars stands for three-quarters of an hour in the hot sun in his own court-yard—he is the incarnation of self-indulgence, but in this book he is shown to have another side too:

Roger Bernhusen de Sars stood there alone, steadfast in his absurdity. The sun blazed on his bald pate, his nose cast a shadow like the gnomon of a sundial, sweat poured more and more profusely, his eyelids blinked more and more slowly as if from drowsiness or help-lessness. There he stood, a living monument to his virtues and his vices.

Hjalmar Bergman knew very well that he was occasionally obliged to defend his abundant use of fantasy, the fantastic element in his art. And he offered an excellent defense indeed. This takes place in the last scene of the Jewish comedy, *The Rabble*—the play he himself aptly called a study of a special gift of fantasy, the Jewish variety. Whether Jews have more fantasy than any other people is probably questionable, but Bergman had many seemingly good reasons to think they did and many funny stories to prove his point in a talk he gave about this play to a group of Jewish academicians.

In any case Joe Meng, the protagonist, is a fantast full of strange and glorious projects. Many of them fail; a few succeed. He himself is in mortal danger on occasion, but he somehow manages to survive. His family, too, achieves a secure inter-mediate plateau, a breathing spell in the harsh world. Meng's old grandmother calls him a fantast as he lies on the floor with his head in her lap after all the violent experiences he has gone through. He replies, (aiming his words at the audience, the world, all of us):

"Fantasy—what do you people want? Doesn't fantasy give you your daily bread? Build your houses? Run your factories? What do wisdom and caution have to offer that fantasy hasn't already invented, possessed, and given you? What are you after, you people, screaming: Look at the fantast! Shame on you, fantast! See how he lives in his fantasies like a prince in his palace. Shame!

"What are you looking for? He is a prince, and one day his palace will be seen by all of you who today are aware only of the rags and the tatters. Look at the fantast!

"He believes he is great and anoints his head with oil, like the son of a prince. What do you want, you people? He is the son of a prince.

And if you succeed in causing his fall and drowning him in your spittle, he will have granted you the privilege of spitting on a prince. He will have ennobled even your sneers. But why sneer? One day his heart will shrivel between fleshless ribs, just as yours will."

CHAPTER 15

Abstention

IN *Arlecchino's Dream* Hjalmar Bergman describes a buffoon climbing to the top of a mountain to become a preacher and a speaker of the truth. In *Jac the Clown* he tells the story of a circus clown who wrote a catechism. These stories undoubtedly reflect some of Bergman's innermost aspiration: to be a preacher, not to say a prophet.

His first known unpublished drama was about penitence. His first published work was a passion play, *Mary, Mother of Jesus*. The pinnacle of his youthful production was *Savonarola*, the great novel about one of the world's foremost apostles of penitence. It was published in 1908 when the author was twenty-five.

His desire was clearly to tell the truth, but the truth he found did not seem to resemble conventional prophetic messages. Undoubtedly his philosophy as a young man, his point of departure, so to speak, was a relatively conventional form of Christianity. His essay for the matriculation examination was entitled "A Comparison between Christianity and Mohammedanism." In it, the seventeen-year-old author is revealed as a thoroughly orthodox, decent, and loyal schoolboy. His family were regular churchgoers but showed few signs of genuine devotion. Still, his maternal grandfather was a warden of the church and apparently possessed a degree of personal faith.

And Hjalmar Bergman's boyhood faith did contain an element of passion, an unusual and personal characteristic—a boundless devotion to the Christ of the Gospels (or perhaps, rather, to Jesus the man). He gave evidence of this devotion on numerous occasions, the first time in his famous letter of confession to

158

Ellen Key in 1904, in which he presumably wanted to explain why he had written a passion play.

My most cherished figure in literature and history has always been, is now, and will always remain Jesus of Nazareth. Maybe it is my own Judas heart that made Him seem soft in *Mary*. . . . And yet, was he not soft? A being who endures suffering without hate—is he not soft? To love the wicked and hate their wickedness, that is strength beyond the capacity of man; but is it not also softness beyond human softness?

In his play Hjalmar Bergman contrasts this weakness, this mildness, this good will with the true face of the world, with the cruelty of Jehovah and with the futility of life. It is this tension between the dream of goodness and the chill and harshness of reality that is the source of much of his inspiration.

It seems that his experience of goodness never ceased to be allied with his image of Jesus. Later in his life, he had occasion to write a number of letters to his motherly friend, Ellen Key. One of them was a sort of defense or explanation of the section of *Comedies in Bergslagen* known as *The Dance at Frötjärn*. Ellen Key had apparently sensed an atmosphere of black magic about the characters. In any case, she objected to the "Bergslagen gloom" in many of the anecdotes. So he defended himself in his reply against the accusation of gloominess. He claims to envy Ellen Key's good sense and equilibrium, her unshakable belief in the future, in a new Messiah. He himself is governed by another law:

I believe that a miserable Jewish man lived in Jerusalem one thousand nine hundred and fifteen years ago. He may have been about my age. Sometimes he cried his eyes blind in his longing to see the shining infant Messiah. Don't you believe it? Blind, you see, blind—that's the key.

An irresistible, irresistible stream of these "black magic" figures that you found so unpleasant emerges from my darkness. Well, how do you imagine I found them? Don't you think I would have described them differently—if I could have?

Blind and in darkness because of a surfeit of longing itself—
that is the diagnosis he wanted his friend to accept in November
1915. His "black magic" is rooted in disillusion—and the profound-
ness of the disillusionment was obviously determined by the
light and beauty of the dream. The letter sheds light on the
recurrent theme in Bergman's life, which one might call "fantast
and prophet."

About ten years later Hjalmar Bergman was the subject of a
long essay by Fredrik Böök, a leading Swedish critic. Böök
tried to prove that Bergman was the slave of his fantasies and
that he did not *feel* for his characters. The essay was brilliant,
but undoubtedly missed the point in several important respects.[1]
It claimed, for instance, that Hjalmar Bergman's involvement
in his play about Jesus and the Mother of Jesus was purely
aesthetic. Bergman was in Berlin when he read the essay and
in one of his depressions. Alone and sick, he was living a hectic
night life and hinting to his friends that he was sniffing cocaine.
He rose to the challenge, however, and wrote Böök in a letter:

> You do me . . . a grave injustice when you . . . write "without being
> troubled by religious scruples, this fantast presents Golgotha on the
> stage. . . ."
> This is completely incorrect. All my life—or since I was five years
> old—I have loved one being only: Jesus Christ. How, then, could I
> have made myself guilty of blasphemy, how could I bring myself to
> blaspheme Him: It's possible that my play is so bad that it is blas-
> phemous in substance. But if you only knew how much of the sincere
> heart of a boy was invested in it, you would not have had the heart
> to make your accusation. . . . Nothing could be more foreign to me.
> What am I but a little lad running around with his heart in his hand,
> trying to hide it here, there, and everywhere?

This was written in 1926, when Hjalmar Bergman was forty-
three years old. But he had still not forgotten the five-year-old
child and his feelings. He did not hesitate to identify himself
with the little child.

Unquestionably, this fervent, childish devotion to a figure

he regarded as a symbol of goodness and innocence was one side of his apostolic zeal. It erupted now and again, as if in defiance of his bitterness and disillusionment; it stayed with him all his life.

The other side of the coin was his desire to dominate, his lust for power over destinies and hearts and audiences. There was unquestionably a connection between this lust for power and the occasional outbursts of aggression—an interesting connection. To revert once again to his own testimony about his childhood, we may recall a humorous passage—written with serious intent—in a letter to Ellen Key in 1904:

At the age of five, I began my preaching activity, directed mainly at my favorite sin, which was pride. I was very effective among my mother's servant girls; one of them joined the Salvation Army to avoid the punishments I threatened her with.

This was the same boy who once asked his mother after church: "God, couldn't that be me?"

There is little doubt that it was the element of aggressiveness ("wrath") and lust for power in Savonarola's character that attracted Hjalmar Bergman. When, as an eighteen-year-old, he began to collect material about the remarkable Florentine, he wrote in a letter to an older woman friend: "What I am looking for is a man of the same breed as myself—do I know if there is such a being?" It is true that subsequent letters in 1905 emphasize the mild traits and the martyrdom. "He was a strange man whom one could not help but love. He believed that the Kingdom of God is goodness, love, and compassion." But in a poem from the same period and on the same topic, the stress was on wrath:

> You throw back your cowl
> from eyes that burn redly
> Your world is too base and too narrow
> for all they are longing to find

and later:

> You throw back your cowl
> from the jet-black wrath of your brow

In the novel, *Laodamia,* a woman who had loved the monk as a young man is asked by Vespucci, a more recent love: " 'Was he never wrathful, your friend?' Laodamia's face lit up as she replied: 'You do not know what wrath is. . . .' Vespucci continues: 'I understood that she despised me.' " Namely, in comparison with the monk.

It is with the help of this violent force, this blast of wrath, that Savonarola ruled Florence. That is what defeats the world-wise and skillful politicians in the novel and causes even such men as Sandro Botticelli, the painter, and Pico della Mirandola, the author, to surrender to the religious revival or to go so far as to don the black and white habit of the Dominicans.

The link between preacher, power, and wrath is a character-istically Bergmanian concept, an illuminating combination. At the same time, it is typical of Bergman's evolution that, when the social reformers began to appear in his works a few years later—Krook, the idealistic engineer in *We Books, Krooks and Rooths,* and Loewen, the artist in *Loewen Stories*—they, too, are gentle dreamers who are defeated by reality, outsiders who succeed only indirectly in influencing the world they find so unjust and so ill contrived. Despite his strength, Savonarola, too, was put to death by men stronger than himself.

The significance of the disillusionment that is expressed time and again in Hjalmar Bergman's earlier works cannot be stressed too often or too strongly. The world was truly not as the dreamer or the aspiring preacher wanted it to be. Not only did the play of human wills refuse to obey *his* will; the dreamer himself was unable to live up to his own dreams. He was, he realized, just as bad as the people who incurred his wrath. Prince Solivro in the youthful tale of adventure is of the same breed: he finally comes to understand himself, whereupon his ability to function is paralyzed and he goes under.

Despite his love of Jesus, the young Hjalmar Bergman was never an orthodox Christian. He tried to come to terms with the perverseness of the world through philosophy. He read Schopenhauer as a young man, and the Schopenhauerian influence is particularly noticeable in *Solivro*. He wrote down a few legends about Buddha with one or two references to the Buddhist denial of life and will. His reading of Schopenhauer seems to have given him a strong impulse to "abstain."

All his life he opposed the notion of free will. He even permitted himself small jibes at Hans Larsson, his revered teacher and friend who, in an essay in the 1890s, tried to save this treasure from the mounting wave of pessimism. Eventually, though, he arrived at a rather personal version of the philosophy of freedom: thought is free, will is not.

At an early stage, however, and under the guidance of Hans Larsson, Bergman discovered another philosopher who appealed to him more strongly: namely, Baruch Spinoza. In 1904, three years after his studies with Larsson, he wrote in reference to his ninety-year-old grandmother: "She is still in possession of all her mental faculties. And we discuss our dear Spinoza, whom we both love, she and I." The same devotion is also expressed in his letter of confession to Ellen Key:

"Kant's shrewdness has amused me immensely; Epicurus, whom I scarcely know, has surprised me; Lucretius has dazzled me. Spinoza I love. He has such great, mild, wise eyes. My old grandmother and I have read him together."

It is interesting to speculate what the youth and his grandmother could have had in common in their reading of Spinoza. But it is certain that Spinoza's view—that the universal order is governed by an absolute logical necessity and is completely impervious to the influence of individual wills—must have been in accord with the young man's first disillusioning experience of the world.

Still, Spinoza was a religious man, a man who treasured

goodness. The religious solution is the *amor fati* of the saints, to learn to love one's fate. To learn to abstain from ones own caprices and foolish desires, to see oneself from the perspective of eternity, to confide one's own will to the greater will, which is both God and the universal order. In Bergman's eyes, there may have been a similarity between Schopenhauer's (and Buddha's) doctrine of the extinction of the will to live, on the one hand, and this philosophy of reconciliation and abstention, on the other hand.

In any case, this hypothesis—for Bergman never commented in detail on his reading—explains a part of what one might call the philosophical aspect of his writing.

To understand Hjalmar Bergman's inner development up to the time of the two-volume novel he wrote in 1918, *Memoirs of a Dead Man*—a central work which, as its title suggests, represents either a nadir or a new beginning—it is wise to recall the crisis he went through in the years 1912 and 1913; I mentioned the significance of this stage of his life in the biographical section in the first part of this book.

The crisis may possibly have had its roots in literary reverses; but it is almost certain that personal factors were also involved. He was only twenty-nine in 1912, but he believed he was constantly ill at the time and was deeply depressed. He found it difficult to write. The stories he did produce were strangely introverted and hypnotic: set in a semi-twilight or semi-conscious world and often peopled by insane or otherwise profoundly unhappy, lost souls. Yet some of the works of this period are among his finest, artistically and psychologically—notably *Lady Gunhild at Hviskingeholm*, the novelette about an unhappy marriage in which a sick woman finds her escape in a dreamlife tinged with eroticism.

It is not impossible—in fact it seems probable—that Bergman discovered certain things about himself at this time that he could not accept.

In his sensitivity, his intense fantasy, and his youthful

idealism, he had constructed a marriage that was a fortress without doors. He would live there alone with his beloved, and his beloved would correspond to his ideals of power and love (the ideals which he later came to terms with in *The Legend*). She would be like his arm or his hand; she would belong to him as an object belongs to its owner. And he actually had found a woman sufficiently strong and good-natured and pure of heart to put up with the existence *à deux* he himself had designed.

His jealousy watched over her. The two were almost never separated over a period of more than ten years. They worked, walked, and shopped together. They traveled together and went to the doctor together. It was a strange marriage, but not an unhappy one. He demanded complete submission from his wife, at the same time as he was helplessly dependent on her. She was his defense against the outside world.

The discovery he made was probably that he no longer could live up to the ideal of love he had embraced with such ardor. He felt the need to escape. But he had neither the courage nor the ability to do so. He was no longer sure of his feelings: Lady Gunhild at Hviskingeholm was his *alter ego*: she lived a secret, erotic dreamlife in a struggle with will and duty, and she confused not only son with lover: she mixed up the sexes with one another. And she punished herself. "A life in deceit is an inexpiable crime," Bergman wrote, using an ancient legal phrase.

My hypothesis is that this profound personal crisis further intensified the disillusionment of his youth, the discovery that reality and dreams were incompatible, that the world lacked a foundation. In this situation, the philosophies of disillusionment and denial of free will, which he had studied as a young man, were revived.

As far back as in *We Books, Krooks and Rooths*, Bergman wrote that good will can exist only in a cold and placid and hopeless heart. Even earlier, in *Solivro,* he made up a tale in which the main character was "dead before death" because he found the world a meaningless mess, a set of toys for the Creator, the playful God Almighty. When, after her great tribulation, Lady Gunhild returned to her sombre life of duty, she moved about her big house like a mechanical doll until madness finally engulfed her brain, almost like a blessed release. In *Marionette Plays*, the characters act on orders from forces outside themselves. To Anne-Marie, Mr. Sleeman is life congealed, empty repetition, spiritual death.

It is this continual struggle with disillusionment and the death-before-death motif that culminates in *Memoirs of a Dead Man*. The story is not only a symbolic presentation of the fact that one can "die" before one dies, but also an attempt to cope intellectually with disillusionment itself: with life. It preaches a kind of solution, a philosophy, almost a religion. This is how one dies before death—and this "death" is a spiritual deliverance.

True, this interpretation of the book requires careful reading. But the attentive reader, who continues to the end, will discover that it is not merely the story of a certain Love Arnberg who, after profound disappointments, moves to Hamburg and takes a job as a waiter and general factotum in a strange and vicious house of entertainment. It is the story of a way of finding salvation from life, its sufferings and compulsions. This method consists of seeing through all the "musts" that life imposes on us, of realizing that they are empty and impotent ghosts. But to do this we must abstain from playing the game, abstain from exercising our will, abstain from revenge and from aspirations, elevate ourselves above all the interests and the blind passionate actions which give birth to new blind actions in an endless chain. In short, abstention.

Memoirs of a Dead Man is a veritable house of symbols—a maze of innuendo. The first part is entitled "Arvet och lagen" ("The Heritage and the Law") and is, in a sense, an "Old Testament" part that tells of a Fall and an Original Sin (hereditary guilt). "Leonie, ett mellanspel" ("Leonie, an Interlude") is the story of the disappointment and catastrophe that decide the fate of Jan, the protagonist. Next comes "Arvet och löftet" ("The Heritage and the Promise"), a "New Testament" part which describes Jan's life in hell (the Hotel de Montsousonge) and ends with his deliverance from that place and from the compulsion of his heritage.

In Jan's case, the heritage finds expression in a desire or a duty to take revenge for his sad fate on handsome, arrogant Mikael Arnfelt, member of the enemy family, who stole his bride. Jan is an Arnberg and Mikael an Arnfelt, and as the families are also related, such an act of vengeance would at the same time be family revenge, a deed committed in the name of the family. "Deliverance" from the compulsion means that Jan grasps the unimportance, vanity, and futility of all "musts," including revenge. Jan sells the "Great Injustice" cheaply. Though it is a family heirloom, it also belongs to the conditions of humanity or the great human order, in which the law of retribution is one of the basic principles. At the moment when Jan "sells the family heirloom and abstains from Retribution," he makes his exit from the context of human wills.

Bergman's method in this great novel is far too complex to be examined here in detail, but we may dwell briefly on the notion of "must" and the way in which its power and emptiness are demonstrated.

The first lesson on the subject is given when Jan meets a Stranger (who may be his dead father) in the town of W. Having just experienced the catastrophe of his life, Jan wants to run away. "I want to get out, no matter what the cost. Because I must." The Stranger replies that Must is a poor adviser. A few minutes later we learn that the family black sheep, the elderly drunk Otto Arnberg (who has long been a parasite on his relatives), has become a thief. His justification: "Because I must live." The Stranger laughs: "You see, Jan! Still another who must live!" But shortly thereafter, Otto Arnberg is found dead, a suicide; he could not live with his crime; he "must" die. The Stranger whispers: "Well, Jan? How about that? Can you interpret the sign, Jan, or do you need others?" Jan needs others.

The second lesson is given by a certain diabolical Mr. Hansen, who deals in patent medicines and shady places of entertainment. He explains the mysterious Hotel de Montsousonge to a puzzled Jan, particularly its attraction for blasé upper-class people. He is as wise as the Devil himself and, in fact, plays the tempter's role. He tries to convince Jan that he "must" take revenge. Mr. Hansen succeeds for the time being, partly by telling a lot about himself, a lad who wanted to make a fortune. He had to get rich. He soon discovered that most people are ruled by a "must" and that the trick is to find out the dominant "must" of each individual. This is one way to get rich. Who, for example, are the people who buy patent medicines?

"And suddenly I saw them before me—thousands and hundreds of thousands, millions of them! The endless hordes of bent, shrunken, thin, stumbling, coughing, shuffling, fumbling sick people who must, must, must. Who must get well, who must clutch at every means of recovery, at every faint ray of hope. Who must believe in the unbelievable, no matter in what form it's offered to them."

He describes the swarms of "musts" that surround us like gnats.

"From the very largest: must live, down through innumerable sizes: must love, must hate, must avenge, must keep up with the times, must be honest, must be good-looking, must be polite, down to the most ridiculous and petty, but not the least insistent: must have a drink, must listen to music, must take cold showers, must have yellow shoes, must have a certain wallpaper, must get out of bed on the right side. . . ."

It sometimes seems, Mr. Hansen says, that these musts are "the only living things on earth, and we humans are their dead playthings." This does not stop him from cunningly mentioning the very must that he believes is Jan's driving force: "must take revenge." And he knows all too well which button in Jan's mind to push. "You know that the reason for your present state of apathy is that you withdrew like a coward." He then goes on to recite the long list of the Arnfelts' sins until Jan is boiling with rage. And Jan himself had already said of revenge: "It is almost the only thing one really must do."

Now Jan begins to prepare his revenge. There is to be a masquerade ball at the Hotel Montsousonge, and Mikael is to be shot to death on the same day. Only a few minutes before the ball begins, Jan still believes that he will fire the gun. But then a group of former friends and relatives, who happen to be in Hamburg, gather like ghosts in this house of death. They all stand around muttering about revenge. Suddenly Jan begins to approach his great discovery: they are too much like ghosts, like puppets. He himself is a living, healthy human being, and he goes off to take his revenge. But he is checked by a remark, a reminder. Hadn't his love for Léonie made him promise to watch over Mikael? This kind of a promise is incompatible with revenge; love frees us from the demands of life and will.

Suddenly it dawns on him that the whole group *is* comprised of ghosts. He turns to the man who reminds him of his dead father: "Father, I don't want to. . . ." Ghosts shall not decide his and Mikael's destinies.

A few minutes later, Jan and his father are standing out in the open. Free? Dead? At least not fettered or enslaved men. Free souls, perhaps?

It is clear that *Memoirs of a Dead Man* expresses a philosophy, an intellectual experience. It is also obvious that the symbolism of this particular novel should be considered without reference to the autobiographical element; otherwise, the interpretation would be too restricted. But the relationship between freedom of will and freedom of thought—between human actions directed, as it were, by some remote authority (or by invisible "musts"), on the one hand, and man's ability to abstain, on the other— may seem somewhat obscure when described in such concentrated form. A glance at Bergman's life and the personal problems that beset him will give more meaning to my abstract accounts and summaries.

In *Memoirs of a Dead Man* Bergman was able to summarize and survey a problem that had been on his mind since his first moment of awareness: the discrepancy not only between will and capacity, but also between will and emotion. He even succeeds in differentiating between will, which was obviously under remote control, and reason/emotion, which in another and more intimate sense was a part of the ego and often capable of watching the tricks of the will with astonishment and consternation.

There is evidence in his writings that Hjalmar Bergman often experienced his own impulses, his own passionate will, as counter to his own conviction, his own "thoughts." In most of his miserable prophets and saints, intentions had appeared in jarring contrast to actions—remember the false Cristopher! And it was often the problems of aggressiveness, of deeds of violence, "murderous acts," that served to confuse the ego image and distort the concept of a reasonable world. His "sorrow about his ego" was rooted in this experience. Powerful impressions made by the First World War could only reinforce and lend greater general validity to this way of thinking. Here—in *Memoirs of a Dead Man*—he was able, at least in a story, to eliminate the rebellious, aggressive, violent element from the ego of a human being. He was able to find a way to deliver the thinking "ego" from the world of warring wills, which he either saw as an irrational source of power (as in *We Books, Krooks and Rooths*) or experienced as an oppressive pain (as in *Loewen Stories*).

To see through one's own will is a painful process: he believed he had done so. To abstain from exercising one's will, on the other hand, is to abstain from life, for life consists of wills and willing is involvement itself. This means living death or at least preparation for death.

The terrible years in Hjalmar Bergman's life, beginning in 1912, may have made it clear to him that, with his will and tendencies, he could not live up to the prophetic, pure ideals he had once designed for himself—including, perhaps, the ideal of conjugal love, the strange ethic of love he had created. This discovery threatened to destroy him. He had experienced those years—or parts of them—as "dead," as the depths of despair. Now he had this suffering behind him.

Memoirs of a Dead Man may be seen as a picture of the warring world but also as a message from the author himself. Let me try to interpret its meaning:

"I know what living death is. I have passed through a door, the door to the Hotel de Montsousonge. I have understood my dream and seen that it was at odds with my ideal. I have understood my lust and have abstained from satisfying it. But also: I am therefore finished with life. I have seen through its essence. I am prepared to die. I am free."

It seems to me that Hjalmar Bergman must have experienced this story as an expression of his own situation and that situation as a readiness for death. Here we have the explanation for his calling his subsequent books "farewells."

Sooner or later in every human relationship the time comes to break up. It begins with the decision to separate, the realization that the time is ripe. After that come the actual leave-takings. *Memoirs of a Dead Man* marks the decision itself: the way was paved for the subsequent books, which said "farewell."

It is now easier to understand why, in the next book, Innkeeper Markurell is brought to a point where he is said to "have died." This is said half-jokingly, and afterward the author informs us parenthetically that Markurell actually died of blood poisoning several years later. The death he suffers in the book is clearly another death, the same as that experienced by Jan: death away from will, from his heart's desire. This is why Markurell could be innocuous in the final scenes of the book: panic-stricken at the thought that his son would learn the awful secret, imprisoned in his love like a rat in a trap; wild Markurell, the crocodile, the primitive egoist, was forced, as a wise and chastened man, to allow events to proceed, to allow Judge de Lorche and Wadköping to go on living. His initials throughout the book have been H.H., for Harald Hilding. Now they might stand for His Holiness instead.[2]

Is the world changed? No. It lives on in its cat-and-mouse game, its inexorable interplay of cause and will. But Markurell has thrown in his hand. He is free. The same is true of Grandmother. The world went in another direction than she thought it would. She wasn't as sensible as she had always believed. She can no longer love through the exercise of power—and without power she cannot love at all. Her only path is through total contrition, almost annihilation. She, too, must abstain from her most precious possession: her good sense. No longer in the real world, but only in her imagination can she now meet her beloved little Nathan and pretend with him that everything is as it used to be, that *she* is strong and *he* is weak. And thus love becomes possible. It is true that she is "dead." She is contrite, but also crushed. Strong Grandmother no longer exists. That is the price she has to pay for love.

But the most profound humiliation, the most grotesque and at the same time the most poignant abstention is that inflicted upon Herr von Hancken. Here illusions are destroyed through a fantastic game with a whole series of symbols of emptiness. He is compelled to face the truth about himself, to remove from his brow the coronet which never existed. He too is not only contrite but crushed. But this, together with the moment of his death, is his life's only moment of dignity, of freedom.

"I, Ernst, Carl, Adolph, Count von Hancken, do hereby of my own free will and after mature, lifelong consideration, abstain for the general good from all the honors which rightly belong to me and have never been bestowed on me. All I wanted to be and to become and for which I had a burning desire and a noble ambition, though not the capacity, I now offer to Almighty God. May He create of it a new being of utter perfection, should it so please Him. I came into this world an empty puff of air, and I inscribed my name in water."

Another ingredient of the "abstention" complex is *"besinning"* (used in *The Portal*) or, "acceptance." It implies that the person who wants to come to terms with his or her life stops placing the blame elsewhere. No one else is responsible for one's fate. Terror —and with it acts of violence, aggressiveness—comes in reality from within. It is essential that this truth be understood and accepted. "Insight," therefore, can be regarded as the beginning of abstention and deliverance.

This notion is clearly expressed as far back as in *Memoirs of a Dead Man.* When Jan allows himself to be incited to a renewed desire for revenge by Mr. Hansen's insidious words, he feels as if he were enclosed in a fiery cage of anger and hate. He is close to annihilation. Then Father Johannes's lantern approaches through the darkness (Father Johannes is, of course, an incarnation of Jan's dead father). Jan hears him say:

"Do you remember, Jan, how frightened you were of being left alone when you were a little boy? And how eager you were to hold your mother or someone else by the hand?"

I remembered.

He laughed and said:

"Maybe you thought some horrible murderer was lying in wait for you in a jasmine hedge? Or that a robber had hidden in the plum tree? Or some other cruel, wicked person was lurking behind the dovecote?

"Oh, dear Jan, there was only one cruel and wicked killer in your grandfather's garden, and there is only one cruel and wicked person, robber and murderer in the whole world, You, yourself."

It is this acceptance that is presented with extraordinary perspicuity in *The Portal.* Here, the portal to death is placed in the middle of the stage, and through it Henrik, the deceived and betrayed protagonist, shall pass. Hjalmar Bergman once commented that this play had its origin in a "mortal peril." *The Portal* is a farewell. Step by step, Henrik is detached from life, from politics, from work, from concern for other people's opinions and for the future. Step by step, he moves toward deliverance.

But while he is still alive, his lines read like so many accusations directed at Life, the Creator, and everyone on earth. It is his friend Mikael who is the voice of conciliation, and his laconic replies are delivered with the same regularity as Henrik's biting, sarcastic expressions of thanksgiving. The dialogue resembles an antiphon:

HENRIK: Merciful God, I thank Thee for everything!
           That Thou has created me so that I should hate all other men. That Thou hast given me thoughts so that I should understand nothing. That Thou hast given me pleasures that were sufferings, lust that was a lie and thirst that could not be slaked.

MIKAEL: Yet it was given you out of goodness.

HENRIK: I thank Thee for giving me a burning heart in order to die, hot blood to chill, a strong voice to grow silent, glowing eyes to be extinguished. That Thou hast given me lungs and liver, stomach and spleen to rot away in pain.

MIKAEL: Yet it was given you out of compassion.

HENRIK: I thank Thee for having created me like a stallion or a bull in rut. I thank Thee for having given me semen, so that my foolishness, my crimes, and my sufferings will never disappear from the earth.

MIKAEL: Nor your happiness, nor your strength, nor your piety.

HENRIK: I thank Thee for the wounds in my breast inflicted by my enemies and for the knives plunged in my back by my friends.

MIKAEL: And what did you learn from all this?

HENRIK: (angered)   That wolves run in packs as meek as lambs, but men run in packs as savage as wolves!

MIKAEL: Why did you join the pack? Were you a wolf yourself?

HENRIK: Thank the Lord, I was a wolf! And now in the embrace
            of death, I regret every good deed and decent act, every
            mild and compassionate gesture in my life.

MIKAEL: Yet it was only then that you truly lived.

It is in this play that Bergman expresses a thought of cardinal
significance which may be regarded as the motto for all his subsequent writings. He also uses one or two key words, in addition
to "acceptance" and "abstention." Forgiveness is one, but forgiveness is not always presented as a possibility. One of the
characters in *Jonas and Helen* is lying on his deathbed. Of him
it is said: "On our long, burdensome journey, we are allowed
only one real victory: confession." This term, too, is a key word.
But in *The Portal* the word is "acceptance," and Henrik does
not realize that he himself is to blame for the complications and
miseries that have beset him until he has passed through the
portal on the stage.

HENRIK: I learned, Mikael, that when an act of treachery was com-
            mitted, I was the traitor. No one else—
            I learned, Mikael, that when I was cheated by life, I was
            the cheat, not life.

MIKAEL: Who allows us to suffer, who brings us disgust in such a
            beautiful place, if not ourselves? Who muddies our happi-
            ness, who betrays our trust, who thwarts our hopes, who
            insults our faith, if not ourselves . . . ?
            Henrik, life is acceptance, coming to one's senses.
            Life is not days and years, not youth, manhood and old
            age, not struggle and strife, not actions and deeds.
            Life is coming to one's senses.

Hjalmar Bergman's mind was like quicksilver. The agility of
his intellect, his daring flights of fancy, his unpredictable trains
of thought—probably founded in the tortured disharmony that
was his secret hallmark—make it difficult to pin down his view
of life. He was not a true disciple of Schopenhauer—far from it.

He was not even a true follower of Spinoza. Nor was he an orthodox Christian.

Yet, as I have attempted to show, there were elements of all three schools in his philosophy—or rather, perhaps, in his life mood. "*Besinning*" or "acceptance" was one term he could find in Spinoza, but it was also a key concept in the Swedish philosopher who was Bergman's teacher as a young man and who he never ceased to revere: namely, Hans Larsson. Father Johannes who, in *Memoirs of a Dead Man* (usually at twilight), is prepared to offer gentle counsel, can be interpreted as a ghostly incarnation of the dead father, and undoubtedly he also resembles Hans Larsson (Hans is a form of the name Johannes or John). It is, nevertheless, obvious that the idea of "acceptance of insight about one's own guilt" and bearing witness to it could easily be made compatible with the Christian gospel. It was Bergman's old adoration of Jesus Christ that found expression again and again.

There was a time in the 1920s—probably after 1926, the most turbulent and desperate period in Hjalmar Bergman's life—when the author was searching more eagerly than usual for Christian themes, biblical expressions of goodness which he could adapt.

In *The Girl in The Dress Suit* an elderly school principal, with the privilege of the deaf and absentminded, is delivering a monologue for the benefit of a spiteful and domineering old woman who, in her conventional despotism, wants to make a young girl unhappy. The key word in this dialogue is "forgiveness," and death is presented as the only certainty the future holds. "To forgive, the principal repeated absentmindedly, that is the great art and the only aim worthy of pursuit."

In the volume *Love through a Window* Bergman included a biblical legend, "The Girl and the Cunning Bandit," an ingenious, comical, and moving story in a biblical setting about a bandit who is disarmed by a young woman's unwavering and innocent goodness: she doesn't give a though to his crimes or his vices but is concerned only with his hunger and his suffering from a thorn in his foot. The girl's name is Anna. And the last lines of the story read:

The girl Anna grew up, she married, she bore a son. He was called Jesus. He became the Friend of the afflicted, the Sovereign of the merciful.
And a crown of thorns was placed on his brow.

Thus Bergman fitted his fantastic and in many ways surprising story into the evangelical milieu to which, emotionally, he was so strongly attached. In some of these tales he was truly successful in creating a theme of goodness reminiscent of Selma Lagerlöf.

However, we are obviously on the wrong track if we are looking for a basis of Christian theology in these stories. Hjalmar Bergman was too great an individualist and a "fantast" to allow himself to be bound by dogmas or formulas. And his keen sense of life's disenchantment and lack of harmony, its absurd structure and total lack of correspondence with human desires, was so fundamental that he could never find refuge in any philosophy that would answer all his questions. For him, the insurmountable barrier was clearly his firmly rooted conviction that will was not free.

He wrote in a letter to Tor Bonnier, his publisher (after the latter had inserted one or two question marks in the margins of *Memoirs of a Dead Man*):

So, dear Tor, you still believe, in the year 1918, that with a little bit of cunning and stubbornness—or in more formal terms: with common sense and *good will*—we can direct, or help to direct, our own and other people's destinies? I, too, believe in common sense and good will, treasures kept under seventy seals somewhere in the universe. And it's probably belief in their existence that keeps us going in the dance of life, a reflection of a reflection of their glow, which we persist in calling the dawn of a new day.

Thus a kind of attenuated and speculative faith. He went on:

So we continue, always the same and eternal, as figures are eternal. We are cards in the solitaire of the Eternal. The king of spades remains the king of spades (with his gloomily majestic expression and his brow creased in thought); the queen of hearts remains the queen of hearts, no matter how often the cards are worn out and replaced by new ones. And we are the ghosts of ghosts, and the tale about us human beings has to be a tale about ghosts—that is, if one happens to look at the whole scene from a distance.

From a sufficient distance: that must mean from the perspective of the portal of death. The result was not exactly the orthodox Christian view of life. But this was not the first time that Hjalmar Bergman wrote or spoke about "roles." In his ideas of individuals succeeding one another in eternal roles, he actually anticipated the psychologists and sociologists of the past several decades, who have found key concepts in roles and the assumption of roles.

Herr von Hancken is built up around the idea of Our Lord's solitaire—that is the foundation of the Reverend Carlander's "universal explanation" or theodicy. The devil is Our Lord's indispensable handyman. While he occasionally takes it upon himself to re-arrange the Lord's plans—and the cards—when the old man dozes off, the solitaire game proceeds *on the whole* according to higher rules and a higher will. Nevertheless, meaningless evil is still present, and it must be explained. The career of the speculative young theologian Carlander is in fact blocked when the bishop learns of his heretical cogitations.

In the same way Bergman is fully aware that the two "testaments," the testaments of inheritance and promise, which are the main ingredients in *Memoirs of a Dead Man,* would scarcely be approved by any ecclesiastical council. Consequently, the first book bore this ingenious motto: "That the heretics' vain doubts and dreadful fears of the superstitious shall glorify Him, and the wailing of the misled shall sing His praises." (The motto is not a quotation; it was written by Bergman.) With subtle self-irony, the words refer to precisely the message the book is intended to convey. The author calls his own belief heresy. Yet—and this is not unimportant—this heresy *nevertheless* shapes itself as a "glorification of Our Lord."

A letter to his old friend Algot Ruhe, in 1921, contains a passage which proves that Bergman regarded his doctrine of abstention not as primarily religious, but almost as a logical conclusion of experience. The letter is interesting and deserves to be quoted at some length. It begins with a description of a street fight he had recently witnessed from his window in Florence. The time was shortly before Mussolini marched on Rome, when Italy was being torn apart by social conflict.

A revolution on a small scale. Yet, is "small" the right word? When you see from a distance of fifty yards a young man being attacked by a gang of about fifty, clubbed to the ground, forced up over a parapet of the bridge to which he clings in a last desperate attempt to save his life—finally losing his grip (probably with hands crushed by the boots of the mob)—when you see and hear without being able to intervene; yes, what is small? Not evil, certainly, nor helplessness. I revert to my old belief: even if one is not always guilty, one always shares guilt. . . .

And what's the point of it all. I don't mean revolution and counterrevolution, but—childishly enough—life itself. Well, I'll tell you, dear friend—if you want to listen, that is—the point of life and the world is to abstain from life and the world. I am not talking about suicide, even less about Buddhism. On the contrary: it's by learning *to feel* that one should learn *to abstain.* In reality, that's what happens when we "live"—whether we like it or not. Consider how the child grabs everything it sees (not to speak of putting everything in its mouth!); how even the young lad begins to be selective just as he discovers new values; how the grown man continues to make new and more discerning discoveries and, with even greater discernment, to sift out as worthless a great part of the lad's values; and, finally, the old man—what is left to him? Do you know something? Life is simply the hour when we pack our bags. The voyage will be long: it's important to pack with discrimination. First you think you have to take everything; all your belongings are useful or precious. But then you realize that there'll be too much, and so you begin to eliminate one thing after another. I wonder what we'll find useful and essential at the moment the signal is given. A bunch of flowers, perhaps? No, the packing must be done with care and insight. The road to Sirius is long, dear friend, and I suspect that excess baggage is very expensive.

During those last years when his way of life was disorganized, when he was ailing in body and longing for death as a release, Hjalmar Bergman felt the need simply to give expression to his own experience. He wanted to share it with others. Hence the element of sermonizing or of didactic formulations—but based on facts, and always done with self-irony. In 1923 he wrote to his friend Hans Larsson about his conversations with Sven Lidman —who had undergone a violent conversion to Christianity a few years earlier and become a preacher in a revivalist movement. The two men had obviously disagreed with one another—they certainly differed in their beliefs—but there was one point on which they could agree. Bergman wrote:

I have a friend (he himself would probably now say: "I had a friend") called Sven Lidman. For a couple of years—1918 and 1919, I believe— we met relatively frequently to speak of matters of importance to both of us. We often took diametrically opposed stands in these philo- sophical and religious discussions. But we always agreed on one cardinal proposition: Truth is humanity's only guiding star and God's only comprehensible form. To search for the truth with more or less weak vision and to speak the truth in a more or less slurred voice, that is a rule of conduct as simple as it is infallible.

Bergman discovered many remarkable truths about mankind. He revealed cruel depths and violent fears, secret, suppressed drives, and many irrational, terrifying forces. In its general struc- ture, his world was always absurd and filled with disappoint- ments. The devil was swift to appear and to shuffle the cards, to change the rules, to sneak his lies into an otherwise promising game of solitaire. The absurd in Hjalmar Bergman could be served up as heartrending tragedy or as hilarious comedy, or simply as something irreparably destroyed, but it could be sensed in almost everything he wrote. He can never be labeled an idyllist; he was never one to gloss things over. Truth above all, as he had seen it.

Yet he did not want to keep to himself the greater truth he had come upon, a rather unusual discovery: that goodness, too, existed. Not as a fundamental, universal principal, nor as something commonly encountered, but as something undeniable and precious, possibly something just as irrational as joy—and just as impossible to deny. Goodness existed as fragments, and in certain periods of his later years, he considered it a mission to write about its fragmentary traces.

Among the hastily written sketches of his later years, there is a casual little piece entitled "Nu vill jag vara en god..." ("Now I Want To Be a Good...") which typifies the kind of understanding that leads to "acceptance."

A good-natured satire, it deals with a man named Erik Eriksson who one morning awakens with a phrase ringing in his ears which he cannot understand: "Now I want to be a good...." He immediately begins to worry. A good what? Businessman? No, he's that already. A politician? He's that, too. A colonel in the army? Ghastly idea, certainly not. An actor? Out of the question. Obviously the man has some suppressed desire which is now surfacing and demanding expression.

It soon becomes clear that there is trouble between Eriksson and his lover. He is enraged (aggressiveness and jealousy once again), and he decides that she shall be punished: thoroughly! She shall be beaten with a club. While his rage intensifies and their altercation grows more heated, the mysterious words keep going around in his head. Suddenly it is revealed that the young woman is ill, that she is doomed to die—those who have read Bergman extensively may recall that he once wrote a sketch entitled "Döden som läromästare" ("Death as a Teacher"). She has reached the end of her tether; she collapses.

This is a shock to Erik Eriksson. Not until he has watched over his beloved for three days in mounting anguish, not until the "teacher" appears on the scene in person does Erik Eriksson understand how the mysterious and oddly haunting phrase should end. It was so simple.

The missing words were: human being.

In all its casualness, this is a tale of good will. Burgeoning, fragmentary, stifled by zeal, plans, and evasions of all kinds. But, crush individuals, put them face to face with death, arrange things so that it will be *too late*, and the fragments fall into place and turn out to be a part of the foundation of their very life, of their true will, their only genuine aspiration. Presumably all of us are so constituted that every once in a while we want to be a good—what on earth was the word we were looking for?

Before the impulse has had time to crystallize, it disappears into the blue.

Yet it was what we were really—*really*—looking for.

These are the fleeting sparks of hope that illuminate Hjalmar Bergman's "sombre," "bizarre," and "fantastic" writings—that is, the worlds that emerged first from the solitary child's sense of make-believe and later in the grown man's search for uncompromising truth.

Notes and References

Chapter Two

1. Gunnar Axberger, *Den brinnande skogen,* pp. 19–89.

Chapter Four

1. Gunnar Qvarnström, *I lejonets tecken,* pp. 63–65.
2. Vilgot Sjöman, "Leonard Loewens drömvärld," in *Kring Hjalmar Bergman,* Sverker R. Ek ed., pp. 44–70.

Chapter Five

1. In nineteenth century Sweden the peddler was a very familiar figure in the countryside. He carried his entire stock in a pack or a box on his back. A prosperous peddler would have a cart. Such a well-to-do-peddler—perhaps rich—is Mr. Kling in the novel *Mor i Sutre* (Ma at Sutre Inn). Swedish peddlers who usually sold fabrics and gems were said to make up to the women of the farms. Their eloquence of course was an important element of the negotiations; Hjalmar Bergman therefore makes Mr. Kling extremely articulate, particularly before a large audience. He talks like an old-fashioned preacher with many biblical quotations. The Swedish province of Västergötland was the favorite seat of those traveling businessmen. It had long been known for its cottage industries and specialized in fabrics and cloths. The Swedish name for the peddlers, *knalle* (plural *knallar*) probably first appeared in Västergötland, it means "one who wanders (*knallar*) about."
2. Gunnar Axberger, *Den brinnande skogen,* p. 136.

Chapter Seven

1. Gunnar Tideström, "Katt och råtta i några av Hjalmar Bergmans romaner. Ett bidrag till tolkningen av Markurells i Waldköping," in *Kring Hjalmar Bergman,* pp. 185–208.
2. *Ibid.,* pp. 198, 204, 205.

Chapter Eight

1. Sven Linnér, "Chefen fru Ingeborg," in *Kring Hjalmar Bergman*, pp. 209–221.
2. Axberger, *Den brinnande skogen*, pp. 19–47.

Chapter Ten

1. Erwin Leiser, "Hjalmar Bergman och Clownen Jac," *Ord och Bild* (1946), pp. 51–58. Cf. Per Lindberg, *Bakom masker*, pp. 125–152.
2. Knut Jaensson, "Hjalmar Bergmans diktning," in *Essayer*, 1946 (Stockholm, Bonniers), pp. 207–276.

Chapter Eleven

1. Statement by Hjalmar Bergman, "Ett drama lever . . . ," *Samlade skrifter*, Johannes Edfelt ed., vol. 27, *Kåserier och kritiker*, pp. 192–193.
2. Stina Bergman on the genesis of the film, "Hjalmar Bergman intime," *Hjalmar Bergman, Minnen och biografiskt*, pp. 25 ff.
3. Both papers appeared in *Samlade skrifter*, Edfelt ed., vol 27. *Kåserier och kritiker*.
4. The quotation from a letter to Ellen Key, Nov. 29, 1915, in *Brev*, J. Edfelt, ed., p. 109.
5. Örjan Lindberger, "Mor i Sutre," Bonniers Litterära Magasin nr. 1 (1946), pp. 42–44.

Chapter Twelve

1. Per Lindberg, *August Lindberg, skådespelaren och människan*, 1943 (Stockholm, Natur och Kultur).
2. On *Spelhuset*, see Per Lindberg, *Bakom masker*, pp. 82–83.
3. Lagerkvist published his plays of this type under the title "Den svåra stunden," *Teater* 1918 (Stockholm, Bonniers), pp. 7–97.
4. I have discussed this problem in further detail in my book *Sju världars herre*, pp. 425–426. The problem of dating the play is seemingly solved by M. Wirmark in her monograph *Spelhuset. En monografi över Hjalmar Bergmans drama*.
5. Helmer Lång, "Marionetterna i Spelhuset," *Ord och Bild* nr. 4 (1951), pp. 218–24.

6. M. Lamm discusses the message from theatre manager Muck Linden in his article "Mina minnen av Hjalmar Bergman," *Bonniers Litterära Magasin* No. 8 (1951), pp. 586–597.

7. See Lindberg, "Hjalmar Bergman dramatikern" in *Bortom masker*, pp. 55–84. Lindberg writes exclusively on earlier plays than *Swedenhielms*; he clearly considers it lacking in originality.

Chapter Thirteen

1. V. Svanberg, "Hjalmar Bergman," *Poesi och politik*, 2d ed. 1956 (Uppsala, Lindblads) pp. 48–58.

2. Another Swedish novelist later used a similar motif: Gustaf Hellström in *Snörmakare Lekholm får en idé*, 1927 (Stockholm, Bonniers). The social process in question is in Swedish sociological literature often called *ståndscirkulation*, circulation of the classes. In older times gifted sons of farmers or merchants would be helped to an education by rich or learned people. If a young man had a good head for studying, it went without saying that he should become a clergyman. It was often the parson or the schoolteacher who made the suggestion. By about 1900 upward social mobility had increased as the society generally had become more affluent. A merchant, a farmer, a craftsman or—as in the novel—an innkeeper, whose financial status was sufficiently stable (although his social standing was a bit uncertain) might feel that his son deserved a white cap as a status symbol, and so did the rest of the family.

3. I have used "Bergslagen" to refer to Bergman's imaginary province, while Bergslagen (without quotation marks) indicates the geographical area. But it seems not necessary to consistently keep a rule like this.

Chapter Fourteen

1. Hans Larsson, "Hjalmar Bergman," *Gemenskap* 1932 (Stockholm, Bonniers).

Chapter Fifteen

1. Fredrik Böök's essay was reprinted, with a few cautious changes, in his book *Resa kring svenska parnassen* 1926, pp. 195–219.

2. Gösta Attorps, "Markurell och påven," *Markurell och påven* (Stockholm, Wahlström och Widstrand) pp. 30–54.

Selected Bibliography

PRIMARY SOURCES

Samlade Skrifter. Johannes Edfelt, ed. 30 vols. Stockholm: Bonniers, 1949–58.
Brev. Johannes Edfelt, ed. Stockholm: Bonniers, 1964.
"Hjalmar Bergman–Hans Larsson. En brevväxling." *Årsbok.* Stockholm: Hjalmar Bergman Samfundet (c/o Bonniers), 1963.
"Hjalmar Bergman–Victor Sjöström. Brevväxling 1919–21, 1922–29." *Årsbok.* Stockholm: Hjalmar Bergman Samfundet (c/o Bonniers), 1966, 1967.
"Hjalmar Bergmans brevväxling med Albert Bonniers förlag." Tor Bonnier, ed. *Årsbok.* Stockholm: Hjalmar Bergman Samfundet (c/o Bonniers), 1962.
Also smaller works in various yearbooks of the Hjalmar Bergman Samfundet.

SECONDARY SOURCES

1. Studies of Hjalmar Bergman

AXBERGER, GUNNAR. *Den brinnande skogen. En studie i Hjalmar Bergmans diktning.* Stockholm: Rabén och Sjögren, 1960.
BERG, RUBEN G:SON. *Hjalmar Bergman.* Uppsala: Verdandi, 1935.
BERGOM-LARSSON, MARIA. *Diktarens demaskering. En monografi över Hjalmar Bergmans roman* Herr von Hancken, dissertation. Stockholm: Bonniers, 1970: with an English summary.
EK, SVERKER R. *Verklighet och vision. En studie i Hjalmar Bergmans romankonst,* dissertation. Stockholm: Bonniers, 1964: with an English summary.
KULLING, JACOB. *Hjalmar Bergmans människoideal. Några konturer.* Stockholm: SKD, 1964.
LEVANDER, HANS. *Hjalmar Bergman.* 2d ed. Stockholm: Natur och Kultur, 1962.

LINDER, ERIK HJALMAR. *Hjalmar Bergman. En profilteckning.* Stockholm: Bonniers, 1940.

————. *Hjalmar Bergmans ungdom. Liv och diktning till och med 1910.* Stockholm: Bonniers, 1942.

————. *Sju världars herre. Hjalmar Bergmans liv och diktning till och med* En döds memoarer. Stockholm: Bonniers, 1962.

————. *Kärlek och fadershus farväl. Hjalmar Bergmans liv och diktning från* Markurells i Wadköping *till* Farmor och Vår Herre. Stockholm: Bonniers, 1973.

MISHLER, WILLIAM. "A Reading of Hjalmar Bergman's *Markurells i Wadköping.*" Ph.D. dissertation (University of Minnesota, Scandinavian Department), 1971, forthcoming.

PETHERICK, KARIN. *Parodi och stilimitation i tre av Hjalmar Bergmans romaner,* dissertation. Uppsala: Scandinavian University Books, 1971: with an English summary.

QVARNSTRÖM, GUNNAR. *I lejonets tecken. En studie i Hjalmar Bergmans symbolkonst.* Lund: Kungliga Humanistiska Vetenskapssamfundet, 1959.

S:T CYR, IRMA. *Hjalmar Bergman privat.* Stockholm: Natur och Kultur, 1973.

WIRMARK, MARGARETA. *Spelhuset. En monografi över Hjalmar Bergmans drama,* dissertation. Stockholm: Rabén och Sjögren, 1971: with an English summary.

2.   Surveys in Works of Literary History

GUSTAFSON, ALRIK. *A History of Swedish Literature.* Minneapolis: University of Minnesota Press, 1961.

LINDER, ERIK HJALMAR. *Fem decennier av nittonhundratalet.* Part I. Stockholm: Natur och Kultur, 1965.

3.   Bibliographical Works

LUND, EDGAR. "Hjalmar Bergman," *Korta bibliografier II.* Stockholm: Edgar Lund, 1939.

LILLIEHÖÖK, ERIC and HENNING WIESLANDER. Bibliographies in *Årsbok.* Stockholm: Hjalmar Bergman Samfundet (c/o Bonniers), 1959–.

4. Recommended Essays and Articles

The following seven essays appear in the volume *Kring Hjalmar Bergman*, Sverker R. Ek, ed. Stockholm: W & W. (1965):

BJÖRCK, STAFFAN, "Komedier i Bergslagen."
EDFELT, JOHANNES, "Hjalmar Bergmans dialog med döden."
EK, SVERKER R., "Marionettspel."
LINDER, ERIK HJ., "Maria Jesu moder."
LINNÉR, SVEN, "Chefen fru Ingeborg."
SJÖMAN, VILGOT, "Leonard Loewens drömvärld."
TIDESTRÖM, GUNNAR, "Katt och råtta i några av Hjalmar Bergmans romaner."

ATTORPS, GÖSTA, "Markurell och påven." *Markurell och påven.* Stockholm: Rabén & Sjögren, 1967.
BERGMAN, STINA, "Hjalmar Bergman intime." *Hjalmar Bergman. Minnen och biografiskt.* Stockholm: Edgar Lund, 1940.
————, "Skall du höra på det här..." *Bonniers Litterära Magasin* 33:6 (1964): 424.
LINDER, ERIK HJ., "Att utforska Hjalmar Bergman." *Bonniers Litterära Magasin* 33:6 (1964): 430.

TRANSLATIONS OF HJALMAR BERGMAN'S WORKS

1. Czech

Markurells i Wadköping	*Skandál v dobré rodině.* Translated by V. Hradečná a L. Jehlička. Prague: Mladá fronta, 1970.

2. Danish

Farmor och Vår Herre	*Farmor og Vorherre.* Copenhagen: Schultz Forlag, 1931.
Hans nåds testamente	*Hans Naades Testamente.* Copenhagen: Kamla's Boghandel, 1918.
Markurells i Wadköping	*Markurells i Wadköping.* Copenhagen: Gyldendalske Boghandel, Nordisk Forlag, 1931.
Markurells i Wadköping	*Markurells i Wadköping.* Translated by Ib Kruuse-Rasmussen. Copenhagen: Borgen, 1972.

Swedenhielms (film version)	*Swedenhielms*. Stockholm: Åhlén & Åkerlund (Bonniers), 1935.

3. Dutch

Flickan i frack	*Katja in rok*. Dr. P. M. Boer-den Hoed. Amsterdam: H. Meulenhoff, 1937. Utrecht: 1952. Antwerp: 1952.
Kurre och Kirre som *skulle vandra jorden* *runt*	*De wråldreis fan Kûrre en Kirre*. A. I. Brouwer-Prakke. Illustrated by Meinte Walta. Drachten: Laver- man, 1963.

4. English

Chefen fru Ingeborg	*The Head of the Firm*. Translated by E. Sprigge and C. Napier. Intro- duction by Dr. R. G:son Berg. London: Allen & Unwin, 1936. Edi- tion: Anglo-Swedish Literary Foun- dation.
Farmor och Vår Herre	*Thy Rod and Thy Staff*. Translated by C. Napier. London: Cape, 1937. (Cheap ed.: 1940).
Herr Sleeman kommer	*Mr. Sleeman Is Coming*. Translated by H. Alexander. *Scandinavian* *Plays of the Twentieth Century*. First Series. New York: American- Scandinavian Foundation, 1944.
Kärlek genom ett fönster and *Labyrinten*	Selections from *Kärlek* ("Can You Cure Me, Doctor?" and "A New Gown") and from *Labyrinten* ("Tri- fles" and "Judith"). Translated by M. Ekenberg. *Modern Swedish* *Short Stories*. Introduction by O. Holmberg. London: Cape, 1934.
Markurells i Wadköping	*God's Orchid*. Translated by E. Clas- sen. New York: Knopf, 1924.

Selected Bibliography

Markurells i Wadköping (the play), Hans nåds testamente (the play), Herr Sleeman kommer (the play), Swedenhielms (the play)

Swedenhielms

Markurells of Wadköping; The Baron's Will; Mr. Sleeman is coming; Swedenhielms. Four Plays by Hjalmar Bergman. Introduction by Stina Bergman. Edited by Walter Johnson. Seattle and London: University of Washington Press, 1968.

The Swedenhielms. Translated by H. Alexander and L. Jones. *Scandinavian Plays of the Twentieth Century*. Third Series. Princeton, N.J.: Princeton University Press for the American-Scandinavian Foundation, 1951.

5. Finnish

Hans nåds testamente

Hänän armonsa testamentti. Translated by Toini Kalima. Helsinki: Kirja, 1923.

Markurells i Wadköping

Markurellien perhe. Helsinki: Otava, 1934.

6. French

Markurells i Wadköping

Les Markurell. Translated by K. Dubois-Heyman. Preface by Lucien Maury. Paris: Librairie Stock, 1931.

Sagan

Une saga. Edited and published by Roger Richard, Av. des Chasseurs, Paris 17. Paris: 1959.

7. German

Amourer:

Amouren. Frankfurt am Main: Anstalt Rütten & Loening, 1912.

Dollar:

Dollars. Munich: Das Werk. Verlag und Betrieb, g.m.b.h. 1935.

En skugga

Ein Schatten and *Herr Sleemann kommt.* Munich: *Das Werk*, 1934.

192

Eros' begravning

Falska papper

Farmor och Vår Herre

Flickan i frack

Hans nåds testamente:

Herr von Hancken

Herr Sleeman kommer

Markurells i Wadköping

Parisina

Patrasket

Swedenhielms

Vävaren i Bagdad

Vävaren i Bagdad
and Porten

HJALMAR BERGMAN

Eros' Begräbnis. Munich: 1934.

Falsche Papiere. Munich: 1918.

Der Eindringling. Berlin: Wegweiser-
Verlag, 1928.

Das Mädchen im Frack. Vienna:
Glöckner-Verlag, 1929.
Katja im Frack. Munich: R. Piper,
1936.

Das Testament Sr. Gnaden. Frankfurt
am Main: Rütten & Loening, 1912.
Das Testament Sr. Gnaden. Berlin:
Ullstein, 1930.
Seiner Gnaden Testament (play ver-
sion). Munich: Das Werk, 1933.

Walter-Verlag, Olten, 1972.

See En skugga above.

Markurell. Munich: Piper, 1935.
Markurell (play version). Munich:
Das Werk, 1935.
Skandal in Wadköping. Translated by
Günther Grass. Afterword by Otto
Oberholzer. Olten: Walter, 1969.

Parisina. Munich: Das Werk, 1936.

Joe & Co. Stuttgart: Munich: Das
Werk, 1933.

Der Nobelpreis. Munich: Das Werk,
1934.

Der Weber von Bagdad. Munich:
Das Werk, 1935.

Der Weber von Bagdad and Das Tor.
Munich: Das Werk, 1934.

8. Icelandic

Markurells i Wadköping

Viðreisn í Wadköping. Translated by
Njörður P. Njarðvík. Reykjavík:
Mál og menning, 1968.

Selected Bibliography

9. Lithuanian

short stories

Paskutinis kavalierius. Translated by Eugenija Stravinskienè. Vilnius: Vaga, 1969.

10. Roumanian

Markurells i Wadköping

Markurell din Wadköping. Translated by Valeriu Munteanu and Paul Anghel. Bucharest: Univers, 1964.

11. Russian

Markurells i Wadköping

Markurelly iz Vadčepinga. Translated by N. Karinkeva. Moscow: Goslitizdat, 1959.

12. Serbian

Chefen fru Ingeborg

Sef gospodja Ingeborg. Translated by Mara V. Nešković. Belgrade: Rad, no year.

Markurells i Wadköping

Markureli. Translated by Mara Nešković. Belgrade: Rad, 1959.

13. Spanish

Swedenhielms

La familia Swedenhielm. Translated by Amada Abillo and Luis Escobar Bareño. *Teatro sueco contemporáneo.* Madrid: Aguila, 1960.

Index

(Works of Bergman are listed under his name)